WE ARE THE CHURCH

52 Second Lesson Text Children's Object Lessons

Wesley T. Runk

CSS Publishing Company, Inc.
Lima, Ohio

WE ARE THE CHURCH

Copyright 1994
The CSS Publishing Company, Inc.
Lima, Ohio

All rights reserved. No part of this publication may be reproduced, stored in a retrieval system, or transmitted in any form or by any means, electronic, mechanical, photocopying, recording, or otherwise, without the prior permission of the publisher. Inquiries should be addressed to: The CSS Publishing Company, Inc., 517 South Main Street, P.O. Box 4503, Lima, Ohio 45802-4503.

Scripture quotations are from the New Revised Standard Version of the Bible, copyright 1989 by the Division of Christian Education of the National Council of the Churches of Christ in the USA. Used by permission.

Library of Congress Cataloging-In-Publication Data

Runk, Wesley T. 1934 -
    We are the church: 52 Second Lesson text children's object lessons / Wesley T. Runk.
    p.   cm.
ISBN 0-7880-0100-0
    1. Children's sermons. 2. Sermons, American. 3. Lectionary preaching. 4. Object-teaching. I. Title.
BV4315.R87   1994
252'.53--dc20   94-8316
                                                               CIP

ISBN 0-7880-0100-0   PRINTED IN U.S.A.

Come to him, a living stone, though rejected by mortals yet chosen and precious in God's sight, and like living stones, let yourselves be built into a spiritual house.

— 1 Peter 2:4-5a

Table Of Contents

1	Children Of God	Ephesians 1:3-6	7
2	Members Of A New Family	Acts 10:34-38	9
3	Jesus Our Rock	1 Corinthians 10:1-5	11
4	Don't Fight God's Plans	Galatians 1:11-24	13
5	God's Little People	1 Corinthians 1:26-31	15
6	Jesus Is The Star	1 Corinthians 2:1-5	17
7	Be A Wise Christian	1 Corinthians 2:6-13	19
8	Be A Good Building Block	1 Corinthains 3:10-11, 16-23	21
9	Good Witnesses	2 Peter 1:16-19 (20-21)	23
10	Keep The Lid On	Romans 5:12 (13-16) 17-19	25
11	When Sarah Laughed	Romans 4:1-5, 13-17	27
12	Work On Your Halo	Ephesians 5:8-14	29
13	Keep Your Mind On The Spirit	Romans 8:1-10	31
14	It Will Be Heaven	Romans 8:11-19	33
15	Hosanna To The King!	Philippians 2:5-11	35
16	Keep Your Eyes On Heaven	Colossians 3:1-4	37
17	With All Your Heart	1 Peter 1:3-9	39
18	The Ransom Is Paid	1 Peter 1:17-21	41
19	The Good Cowboy	1 Peter 2:19-25	43
20	We Are The Church	1 Peter 2:4-10	45
21	Be Ready To Talk	1 Peter 3:15-22	47
22	Little Red Hat	1 Peter 4:12-17, 5:6-11	49
23	The Day The Spirit Came	Acts 2:1-21	51
24	Watch Your Words	2 Corinthians 13:11-14	53
25	Put On A Happy Face	Romans 3:21-25a, 27-28	55
26	The Power Of God	Romans 4:18-25	57
27	What A Sweetheart	Romans 5:6-11	59
28	One Good Man	Romans 5:12-15	61

29	Members Of Jesus' Special Club	Romans 6:1b-11	63
30	I Can't Say No	Romans 7:15-25a	65
31	Worth Waiting For	Romans 8:18-25	67
32	Our Big Brother	Romans 8:26-27	69
33	A Special Kind Of Friend	Romans 8:28-30	71
34	Better Than A Shadow	Romans 8:35-39	73
35	Love One Another	Romans 9:1-5	75
36	The Girl With The Curl	Romans 11:13-15, 29-32	77
37	Mister Wise Man	Romans 11:33-36	79
38	One Body In Christ	Romans 12:1-8	81
39	Brotherly Love	Romans 13:1-10	83
40	On The Winning Team	Romans 14:5-9	85
41	A Thank-You Day	Philippians 1:1-5 (6-11), 19-27	87
42	You've Won The Prize	2 Timothy 4:5-11	89
43	God Loved Us First	Romans 3:19-28	91
44	The Winning Team	Revelation 21:9-11, 22-27 (22:1-5)	93
45	You Are Chosen	1 Thessalonians 1:1-5a	95
46	Follow The Directions	1 Thessalonians 1:5b-10	97
47	A Family Of Crooks	1 Corinthians 15:20-28	99
48	A Friend Indeed	1 Corinthians 1:3-9	101
49	Watch For The Lord	2 Peter 3:8-14	103
50	Test Everything	1 Thessalonians 5:16-24	105
51	Keep Your Soul In Shape	Romans 16:25-27	107
52	God's Broadcasters	1 John 1:1—2:2	109

1
Children Of God

He destined us for adoption as his children through Jesus Christ...
— Ephesians 1:3-6, v. 5

Object: The story of Pinnochio; a puppet that looks like a little boy

Good morning, boys and girls. Look who I have with me today! Can you guess who this is? *(Let them answer.)* Those are good answers, but they aren't correct. This little fellow is Pinnochio. Did you ever hear of him? *(Let them answer.)* Today's scripture lesson reminded me of this story.

Once upon a time there lived a nice old man who was a puppetmaker. He decided to work very hard in order to make a puppet that looked something like this little boy here. Well, the more he worked on his puppet, the more he began to wish that he could have a real son, a real little boy of his own. One night, before he went to bed, he looked out and saw a beautiful star. As he looked at that star he made a wish. Can you guess what he wished, boys and girls? *(Let them answer.)* That's right. He wished that he might be given a son of his own. That night, while the old man was sleeping, a great light came shining into his little house. It came to rest on the puppet that the old man was making. Suddenly, the puppet began to come to life! It could move and talk! The puppet was told that if it behaved like a good little boy, it would one day become a real child, just like other children. Then the old puppetmaker would have a son, a real son, named Pinnochio.

Isn't that a nice story, boys and girls? There is a lot more to that story, but I just wanted to tell you a little bit of it because it will help us to understand what Paul is telling us today in one of his letters. Paul says that God decided a long time ago that we were to become his sons and daughters. We were once like Pinnochio here, all stiff and wooden from sin. For many centuries the chosen people hoped that God would keep his promise and send a Savior—someone who would bring us all to life. After many, many years, God granted their prayer. He sent Jesus to our earth to show us how to live. Because Jesus also died for us and rose again, he was able to free us from our sins. We became alive! What was even more wonderful, we became God's adopted children, just like Pinnochio became the adopted son of the old puppetmaker. But Jesus also told us that to be able to join our Father in heaven we would have to live the kinds of lives that Jesus taught us to live. Where do we learn how to do this, boys and girls? *(Let them answer.)* That's right. We learn from our parents, our Sunday school teachers, our ministers, and a lot of other good people. Let's all try to be good children of God this week, boys and girls. Will you do that? Good. God bless you. Amen.

2
Members Of A New Family

...how God anointed Jesus of Nazareth with the Holy Spirit and with power.

— Acts 10:34-38, v. 38a

Object: An Indian headband and baptismal font (or bowl of water)

Good morning, boys and girls. Today is a special day in our church year. On this day we celebrate the Baptism of Jesus. Does anyone know how and when Jesus was baptized? *(Let them answer.)* Well, Jesus was baptized by his cousin John in the Jordan River. His baptism was a lot different from yours and mine, but it does make us think of the day of our own baptism which probably took place when we were babies. Our parents brought us to church and the minister took some water from a baptismal font like this *(Point to font.)* and sprinkled or poured it on our heads. He also said some special words like, "I baptize you in the name of the Father, and of the Son, and of the Holy Spirit." Our baptismal day was very important because it made us members of a new family. Do you know the name of that new family, boys and girls? *(Let them answer.)* Good! Our new family became the church, the family of Christians. Being baptized is like being initiated into this new family. Do you know what an initiation is, boys and girls? *(Let them try to guess.)* "Initiated" is a big word that means you have gone through some tests and trials to see if you are good enough to be a member of something.

Here is something that was worn by a group of people who had to pass a lot of hard tests to prove themselves. *(Hold up Indian headband.)* Do you know what it is? *(Let them answer.)* That's right. This is an Indian headband. Would someone like to try it on? *(Put it on one of the children.)* If you had been a young Indian boy who lived a long time ago, you would have had to do all kinds of brave things to prove that you were a real man. If you passed all the tests, you became a full-fledged member of the Indian tribe. What do you suppose Indian boys had to do to prove themselves, boys and girls? *(Let them answer.)* Yes, they had to go into the woods alone and hunt down wild animals and do a lot of other things too to prove they were not afraid. Once they were initiated, the young Indians were ready to take on all of the harder jobs of the rest of the Indian tribe.

We have to go through a kind of testing, too, in order to prove that we are ready to become Christians. When we are babies, our parents and godparents help us out by promising for us that we will live good Christian lives when we get bigger. Then water is poured over our heads as proof that we are now ready to be members of this church. Today, as we hear all about Jesus' baptism, let's thank God for our own baptism which took place a long time ago. Will you do that boys and girls? Thank you. God bless you all. Amen.

3
Jesus Our Rock

For they drank from the spiritual rock that followed them; and the rock was Christ.
— 1 Corinthians 10:1-5, v. 4b

Object: A rock and a piece of matzo or a cracker

Good morning, boys and girls. Our scripture lesson for today reminded me of one of the stories of the Old Testament — the story of Moses and the chosen people, wandering in the desert for 40 years. Do you all know who Moses was? *(Let them answer.)* Moses lived many hundreds of years ago. God chose him to help the Israelites escape from Egypt where they were being held as slaves. On their way back home to the promised land, Moses led the people through a desert. Do you think it would have been fun to walk through a desert, boys and girls? *(Let them answer.)* Why not? *(Let them answer.)* That's right. Deserts are full of sand. They are usually hot and very, very dry. Can you guess what the people started asking for and complaining about as they walked through the desert? *(Let them answer.)* That's right. They became thirsty and wanted water. So God told Moses to strike a rock. *(Hold up the rock.)* It was probably a lot bigger than this one! When he struck it, water began to come out of it. Then the people had something to drink. What else do you suppose the people needed, boys and girls? *(Let them answer.)* Yes, they needed food. They grumbled and complained because they were hungry. So God sent them a special kind of bread that looked like this. *(Hold up the matzo cracker.)* It fell from heaven and was called "manna." Would you like to taste this kind of food? *(Break *off small pieces of the matzo and let them try it.)* Don't you think that God was good to the chosen people, boys and girls? He sent them Moses to free them. Then he sent them food and water to get them through the desert.

Today, Paul reminds us that God did the same kind of thing for us. Instead of Moses, he sent us someone else. Who was that someone else that God sent to us? *(Let them answer.)* That's right. It was Jesus. Jesus came to set us free from the power of sin. He did that by his life and by his death on the cross. Jesus also showed us how to get to our heavenly home. He gave us the directions so that we wouldn't get lost. And Jesus left us food for our journey. Do you know what kind of food he left us, boys and girls? *(Let them answer.)* Yes, he gave us Holy Communion, bread and wine, which are signs of his body and blood. He also gave us his word as food for our minds and hearts. Where do we find God's word, boys and girls? *(Let them answer.)* That's right. We find God's word in the Bible, and we hear it read each Sunday during our service. Today, let us thank our Father for all of his gifts to us — especially for Jesus, for Holy Communion, and for God's holy word. God bless you all. Amen.

4
Don't Fight God's Plans

You have heard, no doubt, of my earlier life in Judaism...
— Galatians 1:11-24, v. 13a

Object: A toy horse

Good morning, boys and girls. I brought along this little horse today because I want to tell you a story about a man who got knocked off of his horse one day — by God himself! This man lived long ago — around the time of Jesus. He was a very good Jewish fellow and his name was Saul. The Christians didn't think Saul was a very good fellow, though, because he didn't like them at all. In fact, Saul was very upset when other Jews became Christians. He did everything he could to make trouble for these new Christians. He chased after them, had them put in jail and made their lives as miserable as he could. Everyone knew that Saul really hated the Christians! What do you think of a person like that, boys and girls? *(Let them respond.)*

Well, God must have felt the same way, because one day Saul was riding along on his horse — a horse something like this one — when a very scary thing happened. A great, bright light shone upon him and knocked him right to the ground! Who do you suppose caused that bright light to shine on Saul, boys and girls? *(Let them answer.)* That's right. It was the Lord, himself. Then Saul heard a voice say, "Saul, Saul, why are you making so much trouble for me?" What would you have said to the voice if you had been Saul, boys and girls? *(Let them respond.)* Those are some good ideas. What Saul really said, was, "Who are you?" The voice answered, "I am Jesus." Do you think that Saul was surprised to hear the voice of Jesus? *(Let them respond.)* You bet he was! Besides being knocked off his horse, Saul was also blinded. He couldn't see anything. Jesus really wanted Saul to know that he wasn't at all happy with the trouble Saul was causing the new church. What do you suppose happened to Saul? *(Let them guess.)* Well, the Lord sent a man to help Saul out. This man gave Saul back his sight, and then he baptized him as a Christian. From that day on Saul was given a new name. Do you know what that name was? *(Let them guess.)* Right. It was Paul. From then on, Paul became one of the best Christians, one of the best followers of Jesus. He taught many, many people all about Jesus and helped many, many people to become Christians, also. We thank God for sending the church such a good apostle. Will you try to remember that story about Paul, boys and girls? Good. God bless you all. Amen.

5
God's Little People

...but God chose what is foolish in the world to shame the wise...
— 1 Corinthians 1:26-31, v. 27a

Object: A crutch

Good morning, boys and girls. Today I want to tell you a little story about a boy whose name was Amahl. Does that sound like a strange name to you? *(Let them answer.)* Well, Amahl lived far away across the ocean near the land where Jesus was born. That's why his name doesn't sound quite like yours or mine. Now Amahl was very, very poor. He lived with his mother in a little hut. They were so poor that they had to sell their sheep and their only goat. There was hardly any food in the house, either. To make matters even worse, Amahl was crippled. In order to walk around, he had to use this crutch here, because his one leg wasn't any good at all. Would someone like to come up here and show us how hard it must have been for Amahl to walk around with this crutch all the time? *(Choose a volunteer to try out the crutch.)* If you were crippled, there would be lots of things that would be harder to do, wouldn't there? Can you think of some of those things, boys and girls? *(Let them answer.)* Running and jumping, playing ball, dancing — and probably lots of other things, too. So Amahl got a little sad at times because he was poor and crippled.

One day he and his mother had some very strange visitors. Three men, wearing crowns and beautiful jewels and robes, knocked on their door, asking to spend the night. Who do you suppose they were? *(Let them guess.)* Yes, they were the three kings on their way to see the Christ Child! They showed Amahl and his mother the lovely gifts that they had for this child — the gold, incense and myrrh. They also told them all about this wonderful child who would do great things for his people. Amahl couldn't believe his eyes. He began to wish that he could send something to this wonderful child, too, but he was so poor. Then he had a great idea. He decided to give away the only thing that was really his — his crutch! What do you think of that? *(Let them respond.)* Well, as Amahl was about to hand the crutch to the kings, something wonderful happened. He began to walk — all by himself — without his crutch! God had loved his gift so much that he healed him. Amahl was so happy that he hopped and skipped and danced around the little hut. Then he said, "I will take this gift to the child myself." Amahl was just an ordinary little boy, an ordinary person like you and me, but God chose him to show the wise kings how much he loves the poor and weak people of this world, the little folks. Let's all remember this story of Amahl when we think that we aren't smart enough or strong enough or cute enough. God loves us just as we are. Will you remember that, boys and girls? Good. God bless you. Amen.

6
Jesus Is The Star

...so that your faith might rest not on human wisdom but on the power of God.
— 1 Corinthians 2:1-5, v. 5

Object: An autographed picture of Miss Piggy

Good morning, boys and girls. I would like you to meet one of my favorite people. You probably all know her name, don't you? *(Let them answer.)* That's right. It's Miss Piggy. Did you know that some people have started a Miss Piggy fan club? One year when all the prizes were given out for the best actress of the year, some people wanted Miss Piggy to win for her part in the Muppet Movie. Are you big fans of Miss Piggy? *(Let them answer.)* A long time ago when Roy Rogers was still making cowboy movies, you could join the Roy Rogers' fan club. Every Saturday the movie theater would have a special showing of those Roy Rogers' cowboy movies and all his fans would come. When people really like a movie star or a football player or a singer, they usually try to get that person's picture and autograph. Did you ever get anyone's autograph? *(Let them answer.)*

Did you know that way back in the time of Jesus and the Apostles, people had fan clubs, too? Well, they did! Paul tells us about them in the lesson we will hear today. The Christians started deciding which Apostles they liked best. Some of them liked a man named Apollos, so they called themselves his followers — or fans. Others liked the Apostle Peter, so they called him their special leader. And then there were other people who thought Paul was the greatest. They joined his fan club. How do you suppose Paul felt about all of this, boys and girls? *(Let them answer.)* He didn't like it one bit! Paul said that there is only one person that all Christians should follow. Can you tell me who that is, boys and girls? *(Let them answer.)* Right! Jesus is our leader. Peter and Paul and the other Apostles didn't want to start fan clubs. They wanted to lead people to Jesus. Do you think Paul had the right idea, boys and girls? *(Let them answer.)* He sure did. I want you to remember his words when you see your favorite movie star or football player or singer again. The only person we Christians should follow is Jesus. Let's all try to do that this week. God bless you all. Amen.

7
Be A Wise Christian

But we speak God's wisdom, secret and hidden, which God decreed before the ages for our glory.
— 1 Corinthians 2:6-13, v. 7

Object: A box full of play money (or real money)

Good morning, boys and girls. I'll bet you can't guess what I have in this box! *(Let them try.)* No, it's even better than all of that. Here, let me show you. *(Take lid off of box and show them the money.)* That is really a lot of money, isn't it, boys and girls? *(Let them respond.)* What could we do with this much money? *(Let them answer.)* Yes, we could take wonderful vacations, buy new clothes and toys and other good things. We could really have a good time, couldn't we? What would you think if I were to give all of this money away? *(Let them respond.)* Some people might think I was a little bit crazy or dumb if I gave all my money away. Well, one day a very rich young man came to see Jesus. He probably had even more money than this. Anyway, he asked Jesus what he had to do to get to heaven. Jesus told him to keep the commandments. But the young man said that he had already been keeping the commandments for a long time. So Jesus told him that he should give all of his money away to the poor and come, follow him. Would that have been a hard thing to do, boys and girls? *(Let them answer.)* I guess the young man thought it was too hard to do because he went away very sad.

But there are many Christians who have given away all of their money and other good things just so they could follow Jesus. The Apostles and other disciples did that. Many people probably thought that they were pretty dumb for giving up their homes and other belongings, but sometimes that is what it means to be a Christian. Paul tells us today that Christians don't always seem too smart (wise) to other people because they do strange things like sharing their money with the poor, loving their enemies, and staying close to Jesus. But Paul says that real Christians are the smart people because they are following God's word. They are living the way God has asked them to live.

So, boys and girls, if your friends ever think you are a little stupid for coming to church or for being nice to people who need your help, just remember what Paul tells us today. You are being a smart Christian. You are being wise — just like God. God bless you all. Amen.

8

Be A Good Building Block

Do you not know that you are God's temple...
— 1 Corinthians 3:10-11, 16-23, v. 16

Object: A pile of bricks

Good morning, boys and girls. How is everyone today? *(Let them respond.)* I'll bet you are wondering why I have this pile of bricks here! When I read Paul's letter for today, it made me think of brick and stone and all the things we do with them. What are bricks used for? *(Let them answer.)* Good. We use bricks to build all sorts of things, don't we? Fireplaces, houses, all kind of buildings, like libraries and banks and churches. Do you think that bricks are good things to use for a building, boys and girls? *(Let them answer.)* That's right. They are usually very strong. A house or building made with bricks would probably last a long time.

Do you remember the old story about the three little pigs? *(Let them respond.)* Each one of them decided to build a house. Do you remember what the first pig used to build his house? *(Let them answer.)* That's right. One of them used straw. What happened to that pig's house? *(Let them answer.)* The wolf came and blew it all down. The second pig built his house with sticks. What happened to his house? *(Let them answer.)* That's right. The wolf came and huffed and puffed and the house fell apart! But the third little pig was smart. What did he use to build his house? *(Let them answer.)* Right! He used bricks, just like these. *(Point to bricks.)* And his house turned out to be safe and strong.

Today we will hear Paul say that you and I are like the bricks that make up "God's building," the church. In fact, he says we are God's church! That means that we have to be very strong and sturdy parts of the building, don't we boys and girls? *(Let them respond.)* We can't be like straw that will blow away when the winds blow, or like sand that will crumble when a storm comes. We have to be like one of these bricks. How can we be good bricks in this church, boys and girls? *(Let them answer.)* That's right — by coming to our worship service, listening very hard to God's word and to the sermon. We should also pay good attention to our Sunday school teachers and to our parents. Then we will be good, strong bricks for God's church. Will you try to do that, boys and girls? *(Let them respond.)* Good. God bless you. Amen.

9
Good Witnesses

So we have the prophetic message more fully confirmed. You will do well to be attentive to this...
— 2 Peter 1:16-19 (20-21), v. 19

Object: A copy of the Bible

Good morning, boys and girls. Today I have a book with me which you all know about. What famous book is this? *(Hold up Bible. Let them respond.)* Yes, this is a copy of the Bible. We use this book from which to read our lessons each Sunday, don't we, boys and girls? Does anyone know when the Bible is used for something besides reading? *(Let them guess.)* Well, the Bible is used in a court of law. If you ever have to go to court to be a witness in somebody's trial, you will have to put your hand on this book and swear that you are telling the truth in everything you say. Telling the truth would be very important, especially if you were the only person who had seen something happen — like a robbery or an accident. You would be very important because you would be able to tell everyone what really happened.

Today we are going to hear a story about something that happened to Jesus, and only three people saw it happen — Peter, James and John. Those three Apostles saw Jesus' whole body become as bright as the sun. They saw Jesus look like God, and they heard God's own voice saying, "This is my beloved Son." What would you have done if you had been one of the three persons who saw Jesus look like God? *(Let them answer.)* You probably would have done what these Apostles did. You would have told others all about what happened so that they would also believe that Jesus was God. The Apostles were good witnesses for Jesus because they told many things about him that no one else had ever known or seen. Where can we find out about all these wonderful things, boys and girls? *(Let them answer.)* That's right. We can find out about them by reading this book *(Hold up Bible.)* and by listening very hard when it is read to us during our worship service. Let's all try to listen very hard today when the Bible is read to us. Will you do that, boys and girls? Good! God bless you. Amen.

10
Keep The Lid On

Therefore, just as sin came into the world through one man, and death came through sin, and so death spread to all because all have sinned...
— Romans 5:12 (13-16) 17-19, v. 12

Object: A box, decorated to look appealing

Good morning, boys and girls. How do you like the box I have here? *(Let them answer.)* I'll bet you are wondering what I have in it. Who would like to guess what I have in the box? *(Let them guess.)* Those all sound like wonderful things to have in this box, but none of those answers are right. Let me tell you a story about a box like this that had something very, very strange inside.

Once upon a time a man received a beautiful box like this from a stranger. The stranger asked him to keep the box but there was one thing he was never to do. Can you guess what he was not supposed to do, boys and girls? *(Let them guess.)* The man was not allowed to open the box. So he never did. He just looked at it, because it was pretty to look at, but he never, never opened it to see what was inside. One day a friend of his, named Pandora, came to visit him. When she saw the beautiful box, she, of course, wondered what was inside. But the man told her that no one was allowed to open it. Well, Pandora didn't like that at all. So when the man left the room for a while, she looked very closely at the box to see what she could see. Then she heard a tiny voice from inside of the box calling, "Let me out! Let me out!" What would you have done if you had been Pandora? *(Let them answer.)* Well, Pandora let her curiosity get the best of her. She opened the box! You will never guess what she found there. *(Let them try to guess.)* Those are good guesses, boys and girls, but Pandora found something that she probably wished she hadn't. All sorts of evil, bad, ugly creatures came flying out of that box. These creatures were full of trouble and all sorts of other bad things. Pandora had let bad things fly into the world. She should have listened to her friend and kept the lid on that box, don't you think, boys and girls? *(Let them answer.)* Today is the First Sunday in Lent and we hear lots of words during our worship service that have to do with sin and death — things like Pandora let out of the box. During this time of Lent we Christians all try a little harder to get rid of the bad things flying around in our world by doing good things instead. We would like even you boys and girls to help all of us get rid of sin in the world by living especially good lives during Lent. Would you all be willing to try to be a little bit better this week? *(Let them answer.)* Good. Thank you, boys and girls, and God bless you. Amen.

11
When Sarah Laughed

What then are we to say was gained by Abraham, our ancestor according to the flesh?
— Romans 4:1-5, 13-17, v. 1

Object: A picture of an old man with a beard

Good morning, boys and girls. Today I would like you to meet an old friend of mine who lived a long time ago. His name was Abraham. Did you ever hear of him? *(Let them answer.)* Good. Abraham lived a long, long time before Jesus was born. He was a person very special to God. One day God asked him to leave his home and to travel to a new land which God was going to give to him. What would you have done if God had asked you to go far away to a new land, boys and girls? *(Let them answer.)* Good! Well, you know in those days they didn't have buses or trains or cars or airplanes. So how did Abraham have to travel? *(Let them answer.)* That's right. He either walked or rode on an animal to get where he was going. Abraham packed up all of his belongings, his animals, and, together with his wife Sarah and his nephew Lot, he went to the new land that God was going to give him.

God loved Abraham very much and told him that he was going to be the Father of the chosen people. But one thing made Abraham sad. He didn't have any children. You see, Sarah and he were very old, old enough to be grandparents. But God told Abraham that Sarah would have a son. When Sarah heard that, she laughed! Can you guess what happened, boys and girls? *(Let them answer.)* Right! Sarah *did* give birth to a son. They named him Isaac and loved him very much because he was the only child they would ever have.

What are some of the good things we can learn from the story of Abraham, boys and girls? *(Let them answer.)* Yes, we learn that we should do what God asks us to do. We also learn that sometimes God surprises us with special gifts, like he surprised Abraham and Sarah with a new son. Most of all, we learn that we should trust God because he is our best helper. Let's try to remember all of those good lessons this week, boys and girls. Will you do that? Good. God bless you. Amen.

12
Work On Your Halo

Try to find out what is pleasing to the Lord.
— Ephesians 5:8-14, v. 10

Object: Two little girls, one with a halo and one with horns

Good morning, boys and girls. Today I want to tell you a story about two little girls. But first, I need to ask two of you girls to come up here and be part of my story. Who would like to help me with this story? *(Choose two little girls. Put halo and horn headbands on each one.)*

Once upon a time there were two little girls who were sisters. Their names were Sally and Sassy. Now Sally here *(Point to girl with halo.)* was a very good little girl. She helped her mother with the work around the house and played with her baby brother and paid attention to her teachers at school. She didn't complain when her mom and dad told her to do something, and she never said nasty things about other people. Does Sally sound like a pretty nice girl, boys and girls? *(Let them respond.)*

Now Sassy, her sister, was just about the opposite of Sally. *(Point to the girl with horns.)* Sassy was always getting into trouble. She teased her baby brother until he cried, and she tried to get out of helping with any of the work. She was always getting scolded in school for not doing her homework, and sometimes she even told fibs about her sister. What do you think about this little girl, boys and girls? *(Let them respond.)* Of course, Sally and Sassy's mom and dad loved them both — but sometimes it was much easier to like Sally since she was so good.

Now these two little girls remind us of how we should and shouldn't act toward our heavenly Father. Jesus told us through people like Paul, and he also told us himself, that we should always try to do things that are pleasing to God our Father. Sometimes we all act like Sassy here, don't we? It isn't easy being good all the time, is it, boys and girls? *(Let them respond.)* Will you all try to be a little less like Sassy this week and a little more like Sally? *(Let them respond.)* Good. God bless you. Amen.

13
Keep Your Mind On The Spirit

For those who live according to the flesh set their minds on the things of the flesh, but those who live according to the Spirit set their minds on the things of the Spirit.
— Romans 8:1-10, v. 5

Object: A basketball

Good morning, boys and girls. Today I want to tell you a story about a young man who became a great athlete. His name was Ervin. He was a little black boy who lived in a poor neighborhood with his family. Most of the time Ervin and his brothers and sisters didn't get lots of presents for Christmas or birthdays because there were too many of them, and Ervin's dad didn't have quite enough money to buy the food, pay the bills, and buy lots of presents, too. However, one Christmas, some of the people who lived in the richer section of town decided to collect gifts for the children who were poor. Well, one of the gifts that came to Ervin's house was this. *(Hold up basketball.)* Do you think that this is a nice gift, boys and girls? *(Let them respond.)* So did Ervin. From that day on, Ervin and the basketball were always together. All he did was practice and practice making baskets. He would go to the school playground when no one was around and spend hours just learning how to throw this ball into the basket. Ervin did that until he was old enough to play on the basketball team in school. He was so good that the team started to win all of its games. When Ervin got to high school he was even better because by now he had been playing and practicing for a long time. Ervin led his high school team to a state championship in basketball. Everyone was very proud of Ervin — especially his family, which was still very poor. By the time Ervin was ready to graduate from high school, lots of colleges all over the country wanted Ervin to come to their school just to play basketball for them. Ervin was offered many scholarships. When he finally made his decision, it was even on television because he had become so famous. Ervin eventually became a professional player and started making enough money so that he could help out his poor family back home. That made him happiest of all. Ervin was able to do all of these things because he had practiced very hard all of his life. Do you think it would be hard to practice as much as Ervin did, boys and girls? *(Let them answer.)* It sure was. I told you this story today because it will help us to understand how we are to live as Christians. Paul says that we should always keep our minds and hearts on the Holy Spirit — just like Ervin always kept his mind on this basketball. If we do that, then our lives will be happy and successful in God's eyes, just as Ervin's was successful in basketball. So the next time we see a basketball player, let's remember Ervin — but more especially let's remember the Holy Spirit and how important it is for all of us Christians to keep our thoughts on him. God bless you, boys and girls. Amen.

14
It Will Be Heaven

I consider that the sufferings of this present time are not worth comparing with the glory about to be revealed to us.
— Romans 8:11-19, v. 18

Object: A road sign that says "heaven," with an arrow pointing in that direction

Good morning, boys and girls. How is everybody today? *(Let them answer.)* Today I want to tell you a story about a little girl named Sarah. Sarah was very, very poor. She lived in one of the poor sections of New York City. Her father didn't have a job but her mother worked in a restaurant as a dishwasher. Sarah had five brothers and sisters and the whole family lived in an apartment that had only two bedrooms! Usually, there was barely enough food to go around so you can imagine how hungry Sarah and her family would get! One day, Sarah became very sick with a fever. Her dad tried to take care of her but she just got sicker and sicker. He finally took her to a big clinic in the city where a doctor was able to examine her. The doctor took one look at her and knew she was very sick, so he told Sarah's father that she would have to stay in the clinic for a while until the doctors could help her. Sarah was put into a nice, comfortable bed. But she was so sick and felt so terrible that she just closed her eyes and went to sleep. When she woke up, she was in a strange new place. There was a beautiful shining road in front of her with a road sign like this. *(Hold up road sign that says "heaven.")* She was very curious about where this road would take her, so she followed it until she came to some big golden gates. There at the gate stood a friendly looking old guy with a beard. He smiled at Sarah and said, "Come right in. We've been waiting for you." Sarah went in and saw the most wonderful land she had ever laid eyes on. There were beautiful hills and valleys, flowers, trees, streams, birds, and tame animals. People were everywhere, talking and laughing. One thing she noticed about the people — they all had on shining garments and looked like they were bathed in sunlight. As Sarah looked around, she was overjoyed to see her grandparents as well as her little brother who had died when he was three years old. All of a sudden she realized where she was. She was in heaven! Sarah had died and gone to join all of the other good people in the Lord's special land. There would be no more hunger or pain or fever or sadness. Here there was only beauty — and, of course, the Lord himself.

Don't you think Sarah was a lucky girl to be able to join her friends in heaven? *(Let them answer.)* She certainly was. We don't know if that's exactly the way heaven looks, boys and girls, because Jesus has said that heaven is so wonderful that we can't even imagine it. But it probably is all of those happy, good things rolled into one. Jesus has told us that even though we might have to suffer here on earth, one day we will wake up like Sarah did, with a sign like this one, pointing to God's home. Won't that be a wonderful day for us, boys and girls? *(Let them respond.)* Let's thank God for his great gift of heaven. God bless you all. Amen.

15

Hosanna To The King!

Therefore God also highly exalted him and gave him the name that is above every name.

— Philippians 2:5-11, v. 9

Object: Palm branches, one for each child

Good morning, boys and girls. Today is a very special day for us. We call it Palm Sunday or the Sunday of the Passion. Later on in our worship service we will hear the story of how Jesus suffered and died on the cross for us. We also remember something else that happened to Jesus not very long before he died on the cross. These palms here will help us tell that story. *(Give a palm branch to each child.)*

Today we are going to pretend that you are the crowds of people who walked along the road with Jesus as he went to Jerusalem. Would you like to do that, boys and girls? *(Let them respond.)* Good. Jesus decided that he was going to travel to the city of Jerusalem so he could celebrate one of the special Jewish festivals. His disciples went along, too. Do you know what Jesus rode on to get to Jerusalem? *(Let them answer.)* Yes. He rode on a donkey. As he went along, crowds of people began to gather. They picked up branches, something like the ones you have, and began to wave them. Let's all wave our branches for Jesus, boys and girls. *(Let them wave their branches.)* Then they also started to shout and sing. This is what they said: "Hosanna to the King!" *(Have them all say the phrase.)* Very good! That's just what happened to Jesus when he went to Jerusalem. The people got all excited because they thought he was really going to become their king and rule over them. We know that he wasn't going to do that but the people didn't. They just kept shouting, "Hosanna to the King!" Let's wave our branches again, just like the crowd, and remember that Jesus really is our king — the king of our hearts. And let's shout together: "Hosanna to the King!" *(Have them repeat it.)* Thank you, boys and girls, for helping me out with today's story. God bless you all. Amen.

16
Keep Your Eyes On Heaven

So if you have been raised with Christ, seek the things that are above...
— Colossians 3:1-4, v. 1a

Object: A kite, balloon, flower, candle

Good morning, boys and girls. Isn't this a wonderful day? Do you all know what special festival we are celebrating today? *(Let them answer.)* That's right. Today is Easter Sunday — the day that Jesus rose from the dead. We are especially happy today as Christians because of this wonderful thing that God allowed to happen. Today all of us are supposed to remember that we are special to God, too. We are all going to rise from the dead, like Jesus did, so we should keep our minds on heaven. Paul tells us today that we should always be looking at the things that are above — the things of heaven. To help us do that I brought some things along that have something in common. *(Pick up the kite.)* What can kites do, boys and girls? *(Let them answer.)* Kites can fly high above the ground, can't they? When we fly a kite, where do we keep our eyes? *(Let them answer.)* That's right. We keep our eyes on the kite, up in the sky, because kites usually want to keep going up and up. *(Pick up the balloon.)* Here is a balloon. Balloons have something in common with kites, don't they, boys and girls? What do they have in common? *(Let them respond.)* Balloons like to fly above the ground, too. They help us to keep our eyes on heaven, too. *(Pick up flower pot.)* Here we have a flower. How did this flower get started, does anyone know? *(Let them answer.)* Probably this one got started from a little seed that got buried in the dirt. Pretty soon that little seed began to sprout, and it grew up and up until it reached the air. Then it just kept growing up toward the sky until it looked like it does now. So kites and balloons and flowers all like to reach for the heavens, don't they, boys and girls? *(Let them respond. Light the candle.)* Finally, here is a candle. I want all of you to watch the flame. Which way is the flame reaching? *(Let them answer.)* That's right. The flame is reaching up toward the sky, also. It is sending its little light right up toward the heavens. All of these things today remind us of Jesus' Resurrection, of his coming out of the tomb and reaching up to his heavenly Father. He wants us to remember that we belong up there, too, with himself and with his Father. That's why I want you to think a lot about heaven this week by remembering this kite, this balloon, this flower, and this candle. In fact, you can probably find a lot of other things that keep reaching toward the heavens, toward God. Let's all try to keep our eyes opened for those kinds of things this week — and then praise God for this wonderful day of Jesus' rising from the dead. Will you do that, boys and girls? Good. God bless you all. Amen.

17
With All Your Heart

Although you have not seen him, you love him...
— 1 Peter 1:3-9, v. 8

Object: A great big cut-out heart

Good morning, boys and girls. How is everyone today? *(Let them answer.)* Good. Today we are still thinking about Easter and about Jesus' rising from the dead. We will try to keep Easter on our minds for quite a few more weeks because this is such a special time for us Christians. Today I brought with me this great big heart. It reminded me of some things that Peter has to say in one of our Scripture lessons. What do you think of when you see a heart like this? *(Let them answer.)* Good. We do think of all of those things. Most of all we think of love. The heart is a sign which means "love." That's why we find it on Valentine's Day cards and love letters and other such things. Can you tell me how many different people you really love with all your heart? *(Let them answer.)* Those are very good answers, boys and girls. We love our parents, our brothers, sisters, relatives, friends. We love God, too. Is it a little harder to love God than it is to love your mother and father? *(Let them answer.)* Yes, it is a little harder because we haven't really ever seen God face to face the way the Apostles saw Jesus.

Loving God is kind of like having a pen-pal who lives thousands of miles away. You can read his letters, but since you have never met him, you can only imagine what it would be like to spend some time with him — to get to know him. How do we get to know God? *(Let them answer.)* Good. We get to know God by listening to the scripture readings which tell us all kinds of things about him, about Jesus, and about all that they did for us. We do the same thing with people like George Washington and Abraham Lincoln, don't we, boys and girls? We never met them because they lived long ago. But we read about the good things they did for our country. Then we know they must have been pretty special people. Did you know that your mom and dad loved you before they even knew what you looked like? *(Let them answer.)* That's right. Before you were born, before they knew whether you would be a boy or a girl, they got everything ready for you — your crib, your new little clothes and diapers and all of the things that would be needed to take care of you. They really loved you even before you were born. That is how we love God. Some day we will see him, won't we? When will we see God, boys and girls? *(Let them answer.)* That's right. When we die and go to heaven, we will meet him face to face. But until then, we have to love him without seeing him, just like you were loved by your mom and dad before your birth; just like we admire those people who lived a long time ago. Today I am going to give each of you a little paper heart so that you will remember to try to love God with all of your heart — even though you have never seen him. Will you put this heart in a safe place, boys and girls? *(Let them respond.)* Good. God bless you all. Amen.

18
The Ransom Is Paid

You know that you were ransomed from the futile ways inherited from your ancestors, not with perishable things like silver or gold.
— 1 Peter 1:17-21, v. 18

Object: Several piles of play money

Good morning, boys and girls. How is everyone today? *(Let them respond.)* Good! Do you see what I brought with me today? *(Let them answer.)* That's right — it's money. Actually, it's only play money but it looks a lot like the real thing, doesn't it, boys and girls? What do we do with our money, boys and girls? Can you tell me? *(Let them answer.)* That's right. We use money to buy things that we need. We can also put our money in the bank or give it away to people who need it more than we do. Do you like having money, boys and girls? *(Let them answer.)* Most people like to have money. In fact, we all need money to pay for food and clothing and lots of other things we use every day. People work hard just so they can get money to take care of their families. Money is also used for some other kinds of things, boys and girls. Sometimes kidnappers ask for lots of money. Do you know what a kidnapper is? *(Let them answer.)* That's right. A kidnapper is a person who takes people away from their homes and holds them prisoner. Kidnappers usually make the family pay lots of money to get their loved one back. That's pretty awful, isn't it, boys and girls? *(Let them respond.)*

Paying money to set people free helps us to understand what Jesus did for us. Because of our sin, our father's sin, our grandfather's sin and all of the people who lived before them including the first man named Adam, we were all like prisoners. We needed to have someone come and save us from the power of sin so we could be happy with God in heaven. Jesus wanted to set us free, didn't he, boys and girls? Did he give money like this to set us free? *(Let them answer.)* No, he didn't give money. Instead, he gave his life for us by dying on the cross. That was a wonderful thing that Jesus did, wasn't it, boys and girls? *(Let them answer.)* Whenever we see or use money like this we should all remember how Jesus loved us and gave his life for us. Will you try to remember that this week, boys and girls? Good. God bless you. Amen.

19
The Good Cowboy

For you were going astray like sheep,
— 1 Peter 2:19-25, v. 25a

Object: A cowboy hat

Good morning, boys and girls. Do you see what I have here? This is a cowboy hat, isn't it? Would one of you like to try it on? *(Choose someone to try it on.)* That looks pretty nice on him, doesn't it, boys and girls? How many of you know what cowboys do? *(Let them answer.)* Yes, cowboys do all of those things but the most important thing they do is take care of the cattle. Cowboys spend a lot of time on their horses, making sure the cattle stay together and don't get frightened and start to run away. Boys and girls, do you know how the cowboys kept the cattle quiet during the long nights? *(Let them answer.)* The cowboys would sing to the cattle. This would help to keep the cattle from getting scared. Cowboys really take good care of their cattle, don't they, boys and girls? *(Let them answer.)* If one of you were a cowboy, you would have to be very good at taking care of cattle, wouldn't you, boys and girls? *(Let them answer.)* If one of them got lost, you would have to go and find it. If anyone tried to steal your cattle, you would have to chase the robber away. Most of all, you would want to keep all of the cattle safe.

In the days when Jesus lived, there weren't any cowboys, but there were shepherds. Shepherds took care of their sheep just the way cowboys take care of the cattle. Shepherds didn't wear hats like this, but carried a staff — something that looked like a great big pole or cane. Shepherds also spent a lot of time with their sheep, making sure they were always safe just like cowboys take care of their cattle. That's probably why Jesus called himself the Good Shepherd, so that we would all know just how much he loved us! Jesus is the good shepherd, we are his sheep. Maybe if there had been cowboys in those days, Jesus would have called himself the good cowboy! Then we would be called his cattle instead of his sheep. What would you think of that, boys and girls? *(Let them respond.)* That probably sounds pretty funny to us, doesn't it, boys and girls? But regardless of what he called himself, Jesus wanted us to know that he would take care of us just like shepherds and cowboys take care of sheep and cattle. So the next time you see a cowboy on television, remember what good cowboys do. That will remind you of Jesus and of how he always takes such good care of us. Will you try to remember Jesus — the good shepherd? *(Let them respond.)* Good. God bless you. Amen.

20
We Are The Church

Come to him, a living stone, though rejected by mortals yet chosen and precious in God's sight, and like living stones, let yourselves be built into a spiritual house,
— 1 Peter 2:4-10, vv. 4-5a

Object: Toy building blocks

Good morning, boys and girls. How are you all today? *(Let them respond.)* Good. Do you see what I have with me today? What are these things? *(Let them answer.)* That's right. They are blocks. What do we do with them? *(Let them answer.)* Right. We use them for building things. What kinds of things can I build with these blocks? *(Let them answer.)* Yes, I could build all of those things, couldn't I? What if I wanted to build a church? Do you think I could do it with these blocks? *(Let them answer.)* Why couldn't I build a church with these blocks? *(Let them answer.)* That's right. I don't have enough blocks here. Besides that, I need blocks that are made out of brick or stone. These are too small and too weak to become part of a big building like a church. Boys and girls, did you know that Jesus and his disciples told us what to use when we are going to build a church? A long time ago we were told exactly how to put a church together. We don't use blocks like these, or bricks or wood. Can you guess what we should use to build our church? *(Let them answer.)* Those are good guesses, boys and girls. Jesus and his disciples told us that we are the blocks that are needed for our church! What do you think of that, boys and girls? *(Let them respond.)* That's right. You and I and your moms and dads and brothers and sisters — all of us are the blocks that make up the church. That means each one of us is very important, doesn't it, boys and girls? Let me show you how important each one of us is. *(Build a small pyramid, using your blocks.)* Now, let's pretend that this is our church and that each one of these blocks is one of you. Every time we add one block we come closer to building our church. By ourselves we are only a block but when God puts us together we can be a wall and as he adds more and more we become a great building that Jesus calls his church. You see, boys and girls, that's just how important each one of you is to the whole church. Did you know you were that important, boys and girls? *(Let them answer.)* Well, you are! So let's all try to remember that every time we come to church. The whole church needs each one of us and we need one another. Will you try to remember that, boys and girls? *(Let them respond.)* Good. God bless you. Amen.

21
Be Ready To Talk

Always be ready to make your defense to anyone who demands from you an accounting for the hope that is in you; yet do it with gentleness and reverence.
— 1 Peter 3:15-22, v. 15b

Object: A microphone

Good morning, boys and girls. What do I have with me today? *(Hold up your microphone.)* That's right. This is my microphone which I use for lots of different things. Why do we need microphones, boys and girls? *(Let them answer.)* Yes, we need microphones for all of those things. Usually, when someone puts a microphone in front of you, it means that you are going to say something important that you want everyone to hear. Do you ever watch the news on television? *(Let them answer.)* Good. Do the people who report the news use microphones? *(Let them answer.)* Yes, they do. They especially use them when they want to interview someone who is very important — like a mayor or the President or a famous movie star or sports hero. Reporters often spend a lot of time running after important people just so they can ask them some questions. And when they do ask the questions, they put the microphone in front of the famous person so that everyone will be able to hear what he or she has to say. It would be kind of scary being a famous person, wouldn't it, boys and girls? If you were the President, for instance, reporters would always be following you around and asking you questions. You would have to know what to say because lots of people would be listening to you, wouldn't they?

Well, today's scripture reading reminds us that because we are Christians we also have to be ready to answer questions that people might ask us about Jesus. Lots of people don't know about him, and as we get older, these people will wonder why we go to church, and what we do when we come here. They will have lots of questions for us, and we have to be like all those famous people and be ready with an answer, just as if someone had a microphone under our chin. Would you be ready to answer questions about Jesus, boys and girls? *(Let them respond.)* Well, that's why we come to Sunday school and church. That's why we should listen to what our parents teach us at home. Then someday, when someone asks us about Jesus, we will be ready to give an answer. And just to get ready for that day, I would like each of you to come up here and say your name over this microphone. *(Have each one say name over microphone.)* Thank you, boys and girls, and God bless you. Amen.

22
Little Red Hat

Discipline yourselves, keep alert. Like a roaring lion your adversary the devil prowls around, looking for someone to devour.
— 1 Peter 4:12-17; 5:6-11, v. 8

Object: A red hat for one of the girls to wear

Good morning, boys and girls. How do you like this little red hat I have with me today? *(Let them answer.)* Would one of you girls like to wear it? You can help me tell my story today. *(Choose a girl to wear the red hat.)* Thank you. Now I can tell you my story. It is a very famous story all about a little girl who was very, very nice. One day her grandmother gave her this little red hat to wear. The little girl really liked the red cap so she wore it all the time. Pretty soon everyone began to call her "Little Red Hat." Well, one day Little Red Hat's mother asked her to go and visit her grandmother who was very sick. Now the grandmother lived in the woods about a half an hour from Little Red Hat's house. Her mother told her to be very careful, and most of all, not to leave the path that went through the woods. So Little Red Hat started off, and whom do you think she met on the way? *(Let them answer.)* That's right. She met a big bad wolf who was just hoping he might find a nice tasty girl like Little Red Hat to eat. Well, being a very smart wolf, he asked the little girl where she was going. And since Little Red Hat was a very nice girl, she didn't think he was a bad wolf; so she told him. Then the wolf suggested that Little Red Hat pick some flowers for her grandmother, and Little Red Hat thought that was a good idea. But while she was picking flowers, guess what the wolf did? *(Let them answer.)* He went straight to the grandmother's house, opened the door, and gobbled her up! Then he got in her bed, put on her nightcap, and waited for Little Red Hat to come along. When she got there and saw the wolf in her grandmother's bed, she cried, "Why Grandmother, what a big mouth you have!" "The better to eat you with," said the wolf. And the wolf jumped out of bed and did just that! The story does have a happy ending. Both Little Red Hat and her grandmother are saved from the wolf's stomach by a hunter who was passing by! Now, the reason I told you this story is because it will help us to understand what Peter is saying to us today. Peter tells us to watch out for the devil because he is roaming around like a lion or a wolf, just waiting to get us into trouble. He's just like the wolf in today's story — full of tricks to tempt us into doing what we shouldn't. We are warned by our parents not to sin but often we do so anyway. We disobey God's law and do what the devil suggests to us will make us happy. Thank God for Jesus who rescues us like the good hunter rescued Little Red Hat. Jesus not only teaches us what is right but also saves us from our wrong. Amen.

23

The Day The Spirit Came

All of them were filled with the Holy Spirit and began to speak in other languages, as the Spirit gave them ability.

— Acts 2:1-21, v. 4

Object: A candelabra or several candles in candle-holders

Good morning, boys and girls. Today is a very special day for all of us Christians. Does anyone know what day it is? *(Let them guess.)* Today is Pentecost Sunday. On this day the Holy Spirit came down upon the Apostles. Sometimes we call this day the birthday of the church because on this day many, many people were baptized and became new Christians. Do you remember how the Holy Spirit came? Let's all remember together. It was a Sunday morning, just about like this one, and all the Apostles were gathered together in one place. Do you think that Jesus was with them? *(Let them answer.)* No, he wasn't. Where was Jesus? *(Let them answer.)* That's right. He had gone back to his Father in heaven. Anyway, the Apostles were all together. They were probably praying and talking about how much they missed Jesus. All of a sudden they heard a great big noise which sounded like the wind blowing. How do you suppose that sounded, boys and girls? Can we all try to sound like the wind? *(Have everyone imitate the wind blowing and howling.)* Very good. Then the next thing that happened was really something. *(Stop and light the candles.)* The Apostles looked up and saw flames or tongues of fire, something like the flames on these candles. These tongues of fire were falling right down on them! What do you suppose was happening? Was the roof on fire? *(Let them answer.)*

That's right. It was the Holy Spirit coming to them. The Holy Spirit sounded like a great wind and looked like flames of fire. Would you have been scared if you had been one of the Apostles, boys and girls? *(Let them answer.)* Well, the Apostles weren't scared at all. As a matter of fact, for the first time they were really feeling brave and happy. They were so happy that they all started to talk at once — and guess what happeneded? Each Apostle was talking in a different language! That must have sounded pretty strange, don't you think so, boys and girls? *(Let them respond.)* Just to give you an idea of how that must have sounded, I want each one of you to say your whole name, nice and loud, over and over. And we'll all do it at the same time. Let's try doing that right now. *(Have everyone say his/her full name over and over at the same time.)* Wow, that really sounded mixed-up, didn't it, boys and girls? *(Let them respond.)* Some of the people who came to see what was going on thought that the Apostles were drunk! They weren't drunk, were they, boys and girls? They were filled with the Holy Spirit! Today, on this day of Pentecost, let's all pray that the Holy Spirit will come to us and make us brave like the Christians were on the first Pentecost. Will you pray for that today? Good. God bless you all. Amen.

24
Watch Your Words

... agree with one another, live in peace; and the God of love and peace will be with you.
— 2 Corinthians 13:11-14, v. 11b

Object: A pair of boxing gloves

Good morning, boys and girls. Do you see what I have with me today? *(Hold up the boxing gloves.)* That's right. I have a pair of boxing gloves here. As you know, boxers use these when they fight. Do you think that these can hurt you if you get hit with one? *(Let them answer.)* People who wear these are usually out to hurt another person, so if you don't want to get hurt, it's best to stay away from people who are wearing boxing gloves. Did you know that there is something else that can hurt you even more than these boxing gloves? *(Let them respond.)* Well, there is. Let me tell you a little story and maybe you can guess what it is that can hurt more than boxing gloves. Once upon a time there lived a family — a mom and dad and six children. From the time they got up in the morning until they went to bed again, these people were always arguing with each other. The father usually started it all by yelling at his wife to get breakfast ready. Then she would start throwing things in the kitchen because she was so angry at her husband. When the kids came down to breakfast, the dad would yell at them for being too noisy or too quiet, for not eating enough or for eating too much. They couldn't do anything to please him or their mother. So, when they left for school they started to argue with each other. Either they would steal one another's lunch, or call each other names, or do lots of nasty things that brothers and sisters sometimes do to each other. Do you think this sounds like a happy family, boys and girls? *(Let them answer.)* No, this family wasn't a very happy one. Well, one day there was a knock at their door — and were they ever surprised when they opened it! There stood Jesus. He had come to visit them. In fact, he asked if he could join them for supper. What would you do if Jesus come to visit for supper? *(Let them respond.)* Yes, you would probably be very happy and do everything you could to make him feel at home. Well, this family tried very hard to do just that. When they were all seated at the table, Jesus looked at each one of them and said, "My friends, I have come to remind you of my special commandment. Love one another as I have loved you." Naturally, every person at that table felt very uncomfortable because everyone knew that this commandment had been totally forgotten. The members of this family were not hurting each other with boxing gloves. What were they using to hurt each other, boys and girls? *(Let them guess.)* Very good. They were using nasty words. Words can hurt people more than anything else, can't they? So this week I want all of you to remember this unhappy family and to try very hard to make your own family a happy one. God bless you all. Amen.

25
Put On A Happy Face

...the righteousness of God through faith in Jesus Christ for all who believe. For there is no distinction,
— Romans 3:21-25a, 27-28, v. 22

Object: Two masks, one that looks grumpy and angry, and one that is all smiles

Good morning, boys and girls. I have a couple of masks with me today that I would like to show you. Here is the first one. *(Hold up grumpy mask.)* Would someone like to put this mask on so that we can see how it makes you look? *(Choose someone to wear the mask.)* What kind of a person do you suppose this fellow is? *(Let them guess.)* Yes, this person is just like old Mr. Scrooge. He is always in a bad mood. Whenever anyone comes near him or says anything nice to him, all he says is "Bah, humbug!" *(Have them join you in saying it.)* That's right. So whenever anyone would come up to Mr. Scrooge here and say, "Nice day, isn't it?", he would answer — *(Have everyone say "Bah, humbug!")*. And if someone said to him, "Merry Christmas" or "Happy New Year" or "God bless you," Mr. Scrooge would say, — *(Have everyone say, "bah, humbug!")*. But even worse than that, Mr. Scrooge was very stingy. He wouldn't pay the people who worked for him enough money to take care of their families. Mr. Scrooge didn't care if his workers were poor and hungry. Whenever his workers asked him for a raise, what do you suppose he said? *(Have them answer, "Bah, humbug!")* Right. Well, one night Mr. Scrooge had some terrible visitors — in his dreams. These visitors showed him all the things that had happened to him in the past — how nasty he had been to people — and all the terrible things that were going to happen in the future. These dreams really upset old Mr. Scrooge. In fact, they made him see how all of his nastiness and stinginess were hurting other people. And you know what happened, boys and girls? Mr. Scrooge became a new person — a happy person who looked like this. *(Hold up happy mask. Put it on child.)* Now whenever anyone talked to him, he smiled and said things like, "God bless you." He even gave his workers more money and tried to make up for all of his badness. We would probably all like the new Mr. Scrooge a lot better than the old one, wouldn't we, boys and girls? *(Let them respond.)*

You know, Jesus can help all of us who like to be grumpy to change just like Mr. Scrooge did. When we become a follower of Jesus, we change from grumpy people to good and happy people. We become a little more like God and less like the devil. So this week, boys and girls, let's remember to put on a happy face and to treat others like a good Mr. Scrooge. Will you do that, boys and girls? Thank you and God bless you. Amen.

26
The Power Of God

No distrust made him waver concerning the promise of God, but he grew strong in his faith as he gave glory to God.
— Romans 4:18-25, v. 20

Object: A wheelchair

Good morning, boys and girls. I'm sure you have all seen one of these before. This is a wheelchair and, as you know, it is used for people who can't walk or are too weak to walk. Today I want to tell you a story about someone who spends all of her life in one of these. You might even know about this special person because books have been written about her and a movie has even been made of her life. Her name is Joni. She is a lovely girl. When she was younger, she was very athletic — she liked sports and was a good swimmer. However, when she was a teenager, something very sad happened to her. One day, when she was diving into some water, she hit her head and that accident left her paralyzed from her neck to her toes. What does it mean to be paralyzed, boys and girls? Can anyone tell me? *(Let them guess.)* That's right. Being paralyzed means that you can't move that part of your body. So after her accident, Joni could no longer move her arms or her legs. Can you imagine what that would be like, boys and girls? How would you feel if you had to spend all the rest of your life in a wheel chair, like Joni? *(Let them respond.)* You would probably be pretty sad. Well, Joni was pretty sad, too, for a while. She sat around and felt sorry for herself until one day she realized that she had a terrific friend who could help her out. This person could help her to be happy again, even in this wheelchair. Can you guess who that person is, boys and girls? *(Let them guess.)* Well, those are good guesses, but the person who became Joni's best friend was Jesus! Joni realized that if she put her trust in God and tried to remember all the things Jesus taught us while he was here on earth, then she wouldn't feel so sad anymore. So Joni did just that. Jesus said that we should love our neighbor. So Joni decided to spend time visiting people — especially children and teenagers who were crippled like herself. She went to hospitals and talked to them to help cheer them up. Sometimes she even sang happy songs to them, because Joni had a lovely voice. Joni also learned how to paint by putting the paint brush between her teeth. She learned how to paint beautiful pictures. Most of all, Joni learned how to love God and trust him, and today she is happy even though she can't walk. Let's all try to remember Joni when we don't feel well or when something sad happens to us. Will you do that, boys and girls? Good. God bless you. Amen.

27
What A Sweetheart

But God proves his love for us in that while we still were sinners Christ died for us.
— Romans 5:6-11, v. 8

Object: A great, big, stuffed dog

Good morning, boys and girls. I would like you to meet my friend. Can you guess his name? *(Let children try to guess dog's name.)* Those are very good answers, boys and girls, but my dog's name is Sweetheart! Do you think that is a funny name for a dog? *(Let them answer.)* Why do you suppose I named him "Sweetheart"? *(Let them guess.)* Yes, I do like this dog a lot, but the reason I named him Sweetheart is because this dog loves everybody. He has a heart that must be as big as his body, because this dog thinks everyone is special. If someone were in trouble, Sweetheart would immediately try to help that person. For instance, if one of you fell in a big pool and started to drown, Sweetheart would jump right in and try to save you! Or if you were walking down the street and someone tried to rob you of your money, Sweetheart would scare that person away. One time, Sweetheart saw a little old lady crossing the street. Now this lady couldn't see too well so she didn't notice that a car was coming very fast, right in her direction. Sweetheart jumped between that lady and the car, quick as a wink, and saved the lady's life. Unfortunately, Sweetheart got hurt real bad himself. Sweetheart just loves people, and he would rather give up his life to save another person from being hurt. Would you like to have a dog like Sweetheart, boys and girls? *(Let them answer.)*

You know, all of us have someone who is much better than Sweetheart. This person watches over us and loves us regardless of how bad we are sometimes. Do you know who this person is, boys and girls? *(Let them answer.)* Yes, God, our Father in heaven, is our special friend. He has loved us since before we were born. He loved us so much that he sent us his Son, Jesus. What very wonderful thing did Jesus do for us, boys and girls? *(Let them answer.)* That's right. Jesus gave his life for us. Like Sweetheart here, Jesus wanted to save each of us from the power of sin, so he died on the cross for us. That's why we don't have to wish for a nice watchdog like Sweetheart, here — even though he would be fun to have around. We have Jesus, who loves us, saves us, and shows us the way to our Father in heaven. Let's thank God today for that great gift, boys and girls. God bless you. Amen.

28
One Good Man

For if the many died through one man's trespass, much more surely have the grace of God and the free gift in the grace of the one man, Jesus Christ, abounded for many.
— Romans 5:12-15, v. 15b

Object: Cowboy hats, play guns and holsters, marshal's badge

Good morning, boys and girls. Today I have with me some cowboy hats and some other things that men might have worn in the days of the wild west. People still wear cowboy hats today, don't they, boys and girls? But a long time ago, when the western part of our country was being settled, that's all that the men ever wore. They rode horses and sometimes they carried a holster and gun like this. What kind of people wore guns and holsters in those days, boys and girls? *(Let them answer.)* That's right. The outlaws always wore them. Do you know any of the famous outlaws who lived a long time ago? *(Let them guess.)* Yes, Jesse James, Butch Cassidy, the Sundance Kid, and many others, rode around the countryside robbing banks and trains and people. Do you think the people were afraid of these outlaws? *(Let them answer.)* They sure were! There were big rewards for those who could capture these outlaws, but usually the outlaws managed to get away and keep on making life very hard for the people. Was there anyone who could keep the people safe from men like Jesse James? *(Let them answer.)* That's right. The marshal of the town would try very hard to protect the people by trying to catch the outlaws and make the towns safe. How did the people know who the marshal was? *(Let them answer.)*

That's right. The marshal wore a badge like this. *(Put the badge and a hat on one of the boys.)* When the people saw the badge, they knew that they could trust this person was going to keep them safe from those who were always robbing and killing. Do you remember some of the movies and television shows that were about marshals — or good cowboys? *(Let them answer.)* Marshal Dillon and the Lone Ranger were two of the shows that were all about good cowboys keeping people safe from outlaws.

Whenever we see pictures of good cowboys, we should think of Jesus who was able to free all of us from the power of evil through his death on the cross. We trust Jesus because Jesus was able to wipe out the badness of Adam's sin. He set us free so that we could share in the grace of God, our Father. Because of Jesus, we can all look forward to sharing in the wonderful life of heaven. Let's all remember the Father's goodness to us in sending Jesus, who saved us, taught us how we should live, and gives us the grace to follow him. God bless you, boys and girls. Amen.

29

Members Of Jesus' Special Club

Do you not know that all of us who have been baptized into Christ Jesus were baptized into his death?
— Romans 6:1b-11, v. 3

Object: A sweatshirt or T-shirt that has the name of a club on it

Good morning, boys and girls. Today I have with me a special shirt which you can wear if you are a member of this club. *(Show them the shirt.)* Did you ever belong to a special club? *(Let them answer.)* How do you get to be a member of a club? *(Let them answer.)* Sometimes all you have to do is sign up and then you are a member. Other kinds of clubs are a little bit harder to join. Some clubs make you go through a special test called an initiation to prove that you are good enough to be a member. What kinds of tests do you suppose a person would have to pass? *(Let them answer.)* That's right. Sometimes a person would have to do a very brave thing to prove that he is good enough for the club. Sometimes a person would have to do a silly thing, like wear funny clothes or sing a silly song. A long time ago, two men would sign their names in blood — and that would mean that they were blood brothers. They were members of a special club. Do you think that you would like to be initiated into a club, boys and girls? *(Let them answer.)* Sometimes it is fun, but sometimes you have to do really hard things, and then it isn't fun at all.

Well, there is one kind of initiation that we have all been through and it was a wonderful one. Does anyone know what that was? *(Let them guess.)* We were all initiated as members of the church. Our initiation — our test — was our baptism. When the minister put water on our heads and prayed over us, then we became members of this very special group of people called Christians. We didn't have to sign our names in blood or do anything silly or anything hard. But we did promise, through our parents and godparents, to live as Jesus wants us to live. We did promise to put away all of our bad actions and to live as children of God. Did we get a special outfit to wear when we became Christians, boys and girls? *(Let them answer.)* No, we might have worn a nice baptismal dress, but we didn't get any other kind of uniform. We did get something special for our souls — the wonderful gift of God's grace. This grace helps us to continue each day to be good members of Christ's church. It helps us to be the best Christians we can be. Let's all remember that we belong to this church, boys and girls, and that it was our baptism that made us members. God bless you all. Amen.

30
I Can't Say No

I do not understand my own actions. For I do not do what I want, but I do the very thing I hate.
— Romans 7:15-25a, v. 15

Object: A big plate of chocolate chip cookies — one for each child

Good morning, boys and girls. Look at what I brought with me today. Can you guess what these are? *(Let them answer.)* Right. These are chocolate chip cookies. They are my very favorite kind of cookies. Do you like them, too? *(Let them answer.)* Once I start eating these cookies I just can't seem to stop. One time I ate about twenty of them, one after another! If I do that very often, I will soon get fat, won't I, boys and girls? *(Let them respond.)* I want to tell you about a friend of mine who really needs to lose weight. She weighs about 250 pounds and the doctor has told her that she must stay on a diet, otherwise she will get sick from being too fat. What kinds of things will she have to stop eating if she goes on her diet, boys and girls? *(Let them tell you.)* Yes — all those "fun" foods, like cake and cookies, ice cream, soda pop, potato chips, candy, and probably lots of other things. What do you think would happen if I put this plate of cookies in front of my friend? *(Let them answer.)* She might give in and have a cookie, because it is very, very hard to stop eating all of the things we like to eat. Did you ever try to stop eating cookies and candy and ice cream? *(Let them answer.)* If you did try to give those things up, and someone came along with a great big piece of chocolate cake, I'll bet you would dig right in and eat it! Some of those temptations are just too strong for us. The only way for my fat friend to stop eating is to remember how much better she will feel and how much better she will look when she starts to lose weight. Then, maybe, she will be able to say "no" when someone puts a plate of cookies like this in front of her.

Paul had a lot of trouble saying "no" to temptation, too. In today's lesson, he says that he always seems to be doing the very thing that he knows he shouldn't do — like eating another cookie! But Paul also says that he can remember to say "no" when he thinks about God who saved him through Jesus. God gives him the strength to obey the law and also forgives him when he fails. Today I am going to give each one of you one cookie to help you understand that sometimes we have to say "no" to temptations. And we can do it because God is our helper. God bless you. Amen. *(Pass out cookies.)*

31
Worth Waiting For

For in hope we were saved. Now hope that is seen is not hope. For who hopes for what is seen?
— Romans 8:18-25, v. 24

Object: A large Christmas stocking

Good morning, boys and girls. Isn't this a nice Christmas stocking? *(Hold it up.)* I'll bet you think I am a little strange bringing a Christmas stocking to church in August! Well, I thought this stocking would help us to understand what Paul is saying to us in today's lesson. When you hang your stocking up before Christmas, it is very empty and just waiting for all the treats that will be put into it. Do you ever sit and wonder what will go into your Christmas stocking? *(Let them respond.)* What kinds of presents do you usually find in your stocking? *(Let them tell you.)* This stocking can hold all kinds of wonderful things, can't it? Toys, candy, money, clothes — just about anything you can think of that's not too big to fit. The best thing about Christmas is just waiting for the day to come when the presents arrive because then you can wish for all sorts of wonderful things. And you know that on Christmas Day that stocking will have something in it, won't it boys and girls? *(Let them respond.)*

Today Paul tells us that waiting for heaven is something like waiting for Christmas. We don't know what it is going to be like, but we know that it is going to happen. God has promised that we will all someday be with him in heaven. We believe that just like we believe that we will receive presents in our stocking on Christmas. Even though we have never seen the presents, we know that they will be there. Even though we have never seen heaven, we know and believe that someday we will live there, too. That is a pretty wonderful thing to remember, isn't it, boys and girls? *(Let them respond.)* Let's all keep on waiting for all the good things that will come to us on Christmas — and all of the good things that we will find in heaven. God bless you all. Amen.

32
Our Big Brother

... the Spirit intercedes for the saints according to the will of God.
— Romans 8:26-27, v. 27

Object: Two hats — one that has a sign on it saying, "Big Brother," and one that has a sign saying, "Little Brother"

Good morning, boys and girls. Today I want to tell you a story about two boys. Could I ask two of you to help me with my story? *(Choose two boys.)* Once upon a time there were two brothers. One of them was named "Big Brother" *(Put hat on his head.)* and the other was named "Little Brother." *(Place hat on child's head.)* Now Little Brother really loved Big Brother because Big Brother was always there when he needed some help. One time Little Brother was playing cops and robbers in the living room and he accidentally knocked over one of his mother's very best lamps. It broke into a thousand pieces. What would your mother say to you if you broke her best lamp? *(Let the children answer.)* Yes, she would probably be pretty upset with you, wouldn't she? Well, Big Brother went to his mom before Little Brother could even say anything, and told her what had happened. He told her it was an accident and that he, himself, would help to earn some money to buy his mom a new lamp. Little Brother felt so much better because Big Brother had helped his mother not be so upset. Little Brother was very sorry for what he had done, but he also knew that now his mom wouldn't be quite so angry with him since Big Brother had talked to her first. Sometimes when Little Brother wants to ask his parents for something special like a new bike or some money to go to the show, he doesn't quite know what to say. So Big Brother helps him figure out how to ask for what he wants. Sometimes Big Brother even does the asking for him. It sure must be nice to have someone around like Big Brother, here, don't you agree, boys and girls? *(Let them respond.)*

Today Paul tells us that we all have someone around like Big Brother. Can you guess who that is? *(Let them answer.)* Paul says that we have the Holy Spirit who talks to God for us. He knows how to help us when we want to pray for something special; he knows how to talk to God about the things that are important to us. The Holy Spirit is like having a Big Brother in heaven who carries our prayers to the Father. That's why we should never be afraid to pray to the Father. The Spirit will always be there to make our words come out just right. Will you try to remember that, boys and girls? *(Let them respond.)* Good. God bless you. Amen.

33
A Special Kind Of Friend

We know that all things work together for good for those who love God, who are called according to his purpose.
— Romans 8:28-30, v. 28

Object: A wedding ring

Good morning, boys and girls. Do you know what this is? *(Hold up wedding ring.)* That's right. This is a ring — a very special kind of ring. What kind of ring do you think this is? *(Let them guess.)* This is a wedding ring. Why is a wedding ring so special, boys and girls? *(Let them answer.)* That's right. A wedding ring says that this person is very important to someone else. One person has chosen another to be a wife or husband. That means that these two persons belong to each other — like your mothers and fathers. Some day you will meet a nice person who just might be that special to you. How do you let a person know that he or she is special? *(Let them answer.)* That's right. You do nice things for them. You buy them presents and call them on the telephone and send them cards. When you do all of those things then you let that person know that you really like him or her and that you have chosen that person to be your special friend.

Well, boys and girls, God has done the same thing for us. He has chosen us to be his special friends. How do we know that we have been chosen by God? *(Let them answer.)* We have been baptized into this church. Baptism is one way that God calls us to become one of his special friends. It is like this wedding ring because it says that we belong to God. People who belong to God serve him in a special way. Just as people who are married treat each other with special love, so those of us who love God try to live as he asked us to. How do we know what God wants us to do, boys and girls? *(Let them answer.)* That's right. We read God's word in the Bible. He sent Jesus to help us know all about him. That's why we read from the Bible — the Old Testament and the New Testament — every Sunday. We want to know more about God who has called us to be his very special people. This week, boys and girls, I want you to take a look at the wedding rings which your parents are wearing and remember that we also have a friendship with God, our Father — even though we don't have a ring to show it. Will you try to remember that this week, boys and girls? *(Let them respond.)* Thank you and God bless you. Amen.

34
Better Than A Shadow

For I am convinced that neither death, nor life... nor anything else in all creation, will be able to separate us from the love of God in Christ Jesus our Lord.
— Romans 8:35-39, vv. 38-39

Object: A life-size cut-out of a person

Good morning, boys and girls. I'll bet you can't guess who this is! *(Hold up cut-out of person. Let them guess.)* Those are good guesses but they are wrong. I'll just have to tell you. This is my shadow! Isn't he a nice fellow? *(Let them answer.)* What kind of a person is a shadow, boys and girls? *(Let them answer.)* Right. A shadow belongs only to you. It goes wherever you go, regardless of where that might be. If I go home, my shadow is right there with me. If I have to go to the hospital, my shadow will go along, too. If I am in danger, so is my shadow, and if nice things happen to me, my shadow is there to be happy right along with me. What if I wanted to get rid of my shadow, boys and girls? Would I be able to? *(Let them answer.)* Not really. My shadow is always with me and if I get tired of having it around, that's just too bad for me. My shadow and I are never going to be separated.

Today, in our scripture reading, Paul tells us that the love of God in Jesus is very much like my shadow here. It is always with us. If we are having a bad day, the love of God is right there having a bad day with us. If we don't feel well, or have to go to the doctor, the love of God goes right along with us. If we are happy because it is our birthday, God's love is happy with us, and if we are sad, God is there to help us feel better. The love of God is just like my shadow here. It will never leave us. I could probably tell God to go away if I decided I didn't want him around anymore, but God's love would remain. I could become a really nasty person and do all sorts of bad things — like rob banks, cheat people, tell lies — but God would not leave me. God wouldn't be very happy with me, though, would he, boys and girls? *(Let them answer.)* No — God would rather have us live lives that are filled with good things — good words and good deeds. God's love is with us all the time to help us live those kinds of lives.

Boys and girls, the next time you see your shadow following you around *(Hold up cut-out of shadow.)* remember that there is someone else who is also always with you — the love of God in Jesus our Lord. God bless you all. Amen.

35
Love One Another

For I could wish that I myself were accursed and cut off from Christ for the sake of my own people, my kindred according to the flesh.
— Romans 9:1-5, v. 3

Object: A great big paper heart

Good morning, boys and girls. Today I want to tell you a little story about a boy named Paul who had a brother named Joe. These two boys were pretty close in age and did lots of things together. If Paul decided to go fishing, the first person he would ask to go along was Joe; when Joe wanted to play ball, Paul always joined him. Paul and Joe even studied together and helped each other with their homework. Do they sound like good friends, boys and girls? *(Let them respond.)* Yes, they do. Well, one day, something very sad happened. Joe began to feel very sick. He felt so sick that his parents had to take him to the hospital. At the hospital the doctors found out that there was something wrong with Joe's heart. *(Hold up the cut-out heart.)* Joe had a serious heart problem and the doctors didn't think that he would be able to live. How do you suppose Paul felt when he heard this news? *(Let them answer.)* Yes, Paul was very sad. He couldn't imagine not having Joe around to talk to and play with. So Paul thought and thought about what he could do for his brother. Then he got a very bright idea. He went to his parents one day and said that Joe could have his heart since it was healthy and strong! *(Hold up heart again.)* Would you give your heart to someone else, boys and girls? *(Let them answer.)* Of course, we all know that you cannot live without a heart, so Paul was really willing to give up his life for his brother. Well, in the end, Paul didn't have to give up his heart at all because the doctors found a way to help Joe get better. And the happiest person around, when Joe finally came home from the hospital, was his brother Paul.

That is a good example of brotherly love, isn't it, boys and girls? *(Let them answer.)* Today in one of our readings from scripture, the Apostle Paul offers to give up his own life for the sake of those who are separated from Jesus. Paul wanted everyone to become a Christian, especially those people who were Jews — like he was. They were like his family, so he wanted them to believe in Jesus like he did. But many of them never did believe in Jesus. This made Paul very sad, so he said that he would be willing to be cut off from Jesus if these Jewish people could become Jesus' friends through faith. Paul was a loving person, just like the little boy named Paul in our story today. Both of them teach us a lot about loving others, don't they, boys and girls? Let's try to keep them in mind this week. And God bless you all. Amen.

36
The Girl With The Curl

For God has imprisoned all in disobedience so that he may be merciful to all.
— Romans 11:13-15, 29-32, v. 32

Object: A picture of a "girl with the curl in the middle of her forehead"

Good morning, boys and girls. Does this picture remind you of anyone? *(Show them the picture. Let them guess.)* Those are good guesses, boys and girls, but I'll have to tell you the answer. This young lady is the girl-with-the-curl-in-the-middle-of-her-forehead! Did you ever hear of her? *(Let them answer.)* That's right. When she was good, she was very, very good. But when she was bad, she was horrid! Well, I want to tell you about something she did one day that was pretty bad. This young lady, whose name, by the way, was Tina, had an older brother named Tom. Now Tom had been given a beautiful bicycle for his birthday, and Tom liked that bike very much. He rode it to school each day and to baseball practice and to visit his friends. Wherever he went, he took a chain and a lock for his bike so that no one could steal it when he wasn't looking. Well, Tina really wished she had a bike like her brother's. She would ask him if she could ride it, but he usually said "no" because she wasn't big enough. One Saturday when her brother was gone for the day, Tina decided to take his bike for a little ride. He'd never know anyway, she thought. So she took off on Tom's new bike. She rode up and down the street. Then she decided to visit her best friend, Sally, so that Sally could see this wonderful bike. Tina rode the six or seven blocks to Sally's house, and when she got there, she parked the bike in front and then rang Sally's doorbell. Sally's mom invited Tina to come in, and before she knew it, she and Sally were eating cookies and having a good time. Then Tina took Sally's hand and said, "Come and see what I have." When they went outside, Tina suddenly felt sick. The bicycle was gone! What do you think happened to it, boys and girls? *(Let them guess.)* Yes. It was stolen! Poor Tina. What do you think she did then, boys and girls? *(Let them respond.)* She left Sally and started looking up and down all the streets. She looked and looked, all afternoon. Finally, when it was getting dark, Tina gave up and went home where her mom and dad and brother were waiting. They were very worried because she had been gone so long. Even Tom had been worried. All Tina could do was cry and cry. Finally, she told them what she'd done; she was so miserable that she didn't even care if she got punished. But her brother Tom put his arms around her, and then her father said, "Tina, you can earn some money to help buy Tom another bike. But we are just so glad that you are safe." Tina couldn't believe her ears. Boys and girls, that is how God loves each one of us — even when we're bad. He forgives us, just like a father, and we never have to be afraid of him. Let's remember that this week. OK, boys and girls? Good! God bless you! Amen.

37
Mister Wise Man

O the depth of the riches and wisdom and knowledge of God! How unsearchable are his judgments and how inscrutable his ways!
— Romans 11:33-36, v. 33

Object: A hat or T-shirt that says, "Mr. Wise Man"

Good morning, boys and girls. Today I want to tell you a story about a man who lived many years ago. His name was Solomon. Did you ever hear of anyone with a name like that? *(Let them answer.)* Well, Solomon was a king, and he was a very wise man — one of the wisest who ever lived. When he was first made a king, he asked God to make him wise — or smart — and God answered his prayers. Solomon could have worn a hat like this, that's how smart he was! *(Hold up hat; place it on head of one of the children.)* If you had any special problems, you could go to Solomon and ask him to help you figure out what to do. What kinds of questions would you ask King Solomon if he were here today? *(Let them answer.)* Those are some good questions, boys and girls. Solomon probably had to answer a lot of really tough ones just like that. One day two women came to him with a very big problem. They both said that they were the mother of the same baby! Solomon knew that one of the women was lying, so this is what he said to them. "Bring me a sword. I will cut the child in half and you can each have part of this child." What do you think of Solomon's answer, boys and girls? *(Let them respond.)* What do you think happened? *(Let them guess.)* Well, boys and girls, the woman who was the real mother of the baby told Solomon to give the baby to the other woman. She loved the baby too much to see it killed. That's when Solomon knew who the real mother was; so he gave the baby to her, because she loved it like a real mother would love her child. Solomon was very wise, wasn't he, boys and girls? *(Let them respond.)*

People like Solomon, and other very smart people whom we know, help us to realize how very wise and wonderful God must be. Today we will hear Paul telling us all about God's great goodness and wisdom. Paul uses a lot of big words when he talks about God; but you and I know that Paul just wants us to understand that God is greater than King Solomon and all of the smart and wonderful people who ever lived. Today, let's all praise our great and wise Lord. Will you do that? *(Let them respond.)* Good! God bless you, boys and girls. Amen.

38
One Body In Christ

So we, who are many, are one body in Christ, and individually we are members one of another.
— Romans 12:1-8, v. 5

Object: A family picture album

Good morning, boys and girls. Today we are going to talk about what it means to be a Christian. That's what you and I and all of these people sitting here today are called — Christians. I brought along this picture album because I thought it would help us to understand what being a Christian is all about. *(Hold up photo album.)* This is a very special book. You probably have one like it at home. What kind of book do you think this is, boys and girls? *(Let them answer.)* That's right. It's a book full of pictures. Can you guess who all these people are? *(Open the book and show them a page or two. Let them guess.)* These are pictures of my family! Here are my mother and father. *(Show them. Then point out brothers and sisters and grandparents.)* All of these people belong to me and to each other in a special way, don't they, boys and girls? We have the same last name and some of us look a little bit alike, too, don't we? We are all part of this one, big family.

Paul says that being a Christian is a little bit like belonging to a family like this. You all have the same last name, like Smith or Jones or Edwards, and you might all live in the same house. But each one of you has his and her own name, too, don't you? Each one of you is different from your mom and dad and brothers and sisters. Paul tells us that all of the people in this church have one last name, too.

We all know what that is, don't we, boys and girls? *(Let them answer.)* Yes. We are all Christians. We make up this church. We belong to Christ. But each one of us is special. We each come to church with different gifts. Some of you are good singers; some of you are good at reading; some of you listen very well, and some of you are always helping us out with the work we have to do.

Let's all stand up and join hands, boys and girls, so that we have one big circle. *(Form circle.)* Being a Christian is like being part of this circle. If you weren't right where you are, the circle wouldn't look right, would it? *(Let them respond.)* Let's try to remember how important we all are to this church, but most of all, let's remember who we are. We are Christians! God bless you. Amen.

39
Brotherly Love

Owe no one anything, except to love one another; for the one who loves another has fulfilled the law.
— Romans 13:1-10, v. 8

Object: A nice-looking man's jacket

Good morning, boys and girls. How do you like this jacket I have with me today? *(Let them answer.)* It really is nice, isn't it? The colors are so bright and pretty. Today I want to tell you a story about a young boy who once had a jacket that looked a little bit like this one. The young man's name was Joseph, and he lived many years before Jesus was born. Joseph had eleven brothers. How would you like to have eleven brothers? *(Let them respond.)* Do you think that you would get into a lot of arguments with eleven brothers? *(Let them answer.)* Well, Joseph had a big problem with his brothers, too. They didn't like him very well at all; in fact, they were very jealous of him because their father had given him this coat to wear. Well, one day Joseph's brothers got so mad at him that they decided to get rid of him. Can you guess what they did to him? *(Let them guess.)* First, they were going to kill him, but then they decided, instead, to sell him to some men who were traveling to Egypt. That was a terrible thing to do to their brother Joseph, don't you agree, boys and girls? *(Let them answer.)* You would certainly never do anything like that to your brothers and sisters! Well, Joseph was lucky because God was on his side. Joseph became a very important man in that new country; the king of Egypt liked Joseph. He put him in charge of all the crops and all the workers. One year there wasn't enough food to go around to all the people in other places. Many people were starving. But the people in Egypt had lots of food because Joseph had stored it all up. People from other towns came to Joseph for food. One day, some men who looked very familiar to Joseph came to see him. Can you guess who they were? *(Let them guess.)* They were Joseph's brothers! What would you have done to them if you had been Joseph? *(Let them answer.)* Well, Joseph didn't get even. Instead, he was very kind to his brothers, even though they had been so terrible to him. He gave them food and money. Joseph treated his brothers the way Paul tells us today to treat our neighbor. The only thing we should owe our neighbor is love. Loving our neighbor — and our brothers, sisters, moms, and dads — is the most important law for us to keep. So the next time we get in a fight with our brother or sister, let's remember Joseph and try to love instead of fight! OK, boys and girls? Good. God bless you. Amen.

40
On The Winning Team

If we live, we live to the Lord, and if we die, we die to the Lord; so then, whether we live or whether we die, we are the Lord's.
— Romans 14:5-9, v. 8

Object: A football jersey

Good morning, boys and girls. Look what I have with me today. *(Hold up football jersey.)* Which school is this from? *(Let them answer.)* Would one of you like to wear this today? *(Choose a youngster to wear the jersey.)* How many of you would like to belong to a team someday? *(Let them answer.)* Would some of you like to be cheerleaders for a team? *(Let them answer.)* When you are in school, it can be a lot of fun to go and root for your school team. Everyone gets very excited. The band plays the school song and it marches around the field. Sometimes it's raining or snowing and everyone gets wet and muddy, but still the game goes on, doesn't it, boys and girls? What do you do when your team scores a touchdown? *(Let them answer.)* That's right. You cheer a lot, so that the team will know you are there; you want the team to get excited, too, and score again. What do you do when your team loses, boys and girls? *(Let them answer.)* Yes, you probably feel pretty bad. But you wouldn't "boo" your own team for losing, would you? *(Let them answer.)* No — you might "boo" the other team, but you certainly wouldn't "boo" your own. Your team probably tried very hard to win but the other team was just a little better.

Win or lose, your team is still your team, isn't it, boys and girls? *(Let them respond.)* You wouldn't throw the whole team out just because it lost a game, would you? *(Let them respond.)* No, you wouldn't.

Paul tells us that God treats us a little bit like we treat our football team — only God treats us even better! God wants us to know that we belong to him whether we win or lose, live or die. We are God's. He is the one person who is always on our side. So this fall when we watch a football game or see someone wearing a jersey like this one, let's remember that we belong to an even greater team. We belong to God's people, the church. Will you remember that, boys and girls? Good! God bless you. Amen.

41
A Thank-You Day

I thank my God every time I remember you.
— Philippians 1:1-5 (6-11), 19-27, v. 3

Object: A hand puppet

Good morning, boys and girls. I have a little friend with me today who has a very unusual name. Can you guess what it is? *(Let them guess.)* Those are nice names, but I'll have to tell you his name. It is "Thank-you!" Now that might seem pretty funny, but you see, boys and girls, my little puppet can only say two words. Guess what they are? *(Let them guess.)* That's right. All he can say is "thank you."

Since Thanksgiving Day is just a little more than a month away, I thought today would be a good day to think of all the reasons why we want to say "thank you" to the Lord. I'm going to give each of you a chance to tell "Mr. Thank-you" here what you want to say thank you for. Then he will pass your thank you right on to the Lord. *(Go around the group, allowing each child to name a reason why he/she is thankful. Mr. Thank-you should say "Thank you" after each one.)*

Thank you, boys and girls. Those were some very wonderful reasons to be thankful to the Lord. Today we will hear Paul's reasons for being thankful, too. Paul is thankful for the Christian people who live in the town of Philippi. He is thankful for them because they have helped him spread the news about Jesus. Paul knows that God has given these Christians special gifts so that they can help him with his work. That's why he is saying thank you to God. When we hear Paul say thank you to the Lord, let's all say thank you again just for being here today and sharing in this worship service. Will you do that, boys and girls? Good. God bless you. Amen.

42
You've Won The Prize

I have fought the good fight, I have finished the race, I have kept the faith.
— 2 Timothy 4:5-11, v. 7

Object: A crown, a vase of flowers, a gold cup, a pile of money, candy, and a small prize for each child (lollypop, balloon, tootsie roll, etc.)

Good morning, boys and girls. Look at all of these good things I have with me today. A crown, money, flowers, candy — what do you suppose all of these things are for? *(Let them answer.)* Well, these are all prizes. What is a prize? Can anyone tell me? *(Let them answer.)* Yes. A prize is something you win. Can you think of anyone who would ever win a crown for a prize? *(Let them answer.)* That's right. The young lady who wins the title of "Miss America" receives a crown for her head. That means that she was the best person of all the women who tried out. She could sing or dance better, talk better, and she probably looked very pretty, too. Who would win all this money? *(Let them guess.)* A person who had the fastest horse or car in a race would probably get a lot of money like this. I wonder what kind of a person would get flowers for a prize? *(Let them guess.)* Sometimes a person — especially a woman — who sings very well in a big concert or stage show will get flowers when she comes out to take her bow. A gold cup is given to the best tennis player, and if you won a spelling contest at school, you might get this candy. Did any of you ever win a prize? *(Let them answer.)* That's very good! How many people usually win a prize in a race? *(Let them answer.)*

That's right. Usually only one person wins the prize in a contest or a race. But you know what, boys and girls? Paul tells us today that when it comes to being a Christian, everyone wins the prize! There isn't just one person who gets the flowers or money or gold cup; all of us who have believed in Jesus will win the prize. Do you all know what the prize is, boys and girls? *(Let them answer.)* Right. The prize is heaven. We will all share it with one another. Isn't that a better prize than money or flowers or crowns, boys and girls? *(Let them answer.)* It sure is! Today I want to give you this small prize to help you remember the big prize of heaven. *(Pass out small prizes.)* Amen.

43
God Loved Us First

For we hold that a person is justified by faith apart from works prescribed by the law.
— Romans 3:19-28, v. 28

Object: A baby — a real one or a doll

Good morning, boys and girls. Isn't this a lovely baby I have with me today? *(Let them answer.)* Can you guess what her name is? *(Let them guess.)* Her name is _____. She's a real sweetheart, and you can bet her mom and dad love her an awful lot. Why do you suppose her mom and dad love her so much? *(Let them answer.)* Those are good reasons. Because she's cute, because she's a girl; because she smiles a lot. Most of all, they love her just because she belongs to them.

How many things do you think this baby can do? *(Let them guess.)* She can gurgle and coo. She can cry when she's hungry. She can roll over, and she can sit. She can play with her toys and smile at people and stand up if you help her. But — she can't do very much else, can she, boys and girls? *(Let them respond.)* Babies aren't really good for much, are they? They can't talk and tell you what they want. They can't help with the dishes or pick up their toys. They can't dress themselves. If babies are so helpless and useless, why do we love them so much? *(Let them answer.)* Yes, boys and girls — we love them "just because." You mother and father loved you like that right from the time you were born. Even when you cried all night and kept them awake, they loved you. Even when you got sick and they had to miss a vacation or a special trip, they loved you. Even when you threw your food on the floor or broke your mother's favorite dish, your parents still loved you.

Moms and dads love us just the way God loves us. Even though we don't do very many good things, God loves us. God loved us before we were born; he will love us until we die and join him in heaven. Just as this baby didn't have to do anything to make her parents love her, so we didn't have to do anything either to get God's love. When this baby grows up, do you think it will love its mom and dad? *(Let them answer.)* Yes. And as you and I grow up as Christians, we begin to love God back; we begin to live as he would like us to live. But the most wonderful thing about God — and about parents — is that they loved us first, when we were helpless, like this baby. Today, let's thank God for our parents and for all of the love he has given us. God bless you. Amen.

44

The Winning Team

But nothing unclean will enter it...but only those who are written in the Lamb's book of life.
— Revelation 21:9-11, 22-27 (22:1-5), v. 27

Object: A basketball T-shirt, bearing the name of a local high school

Good morning, boys and girls. Whose T-shirt do I have with me today? *(Hold up shirt. Let them tell you.)* This is *(Name of school)* T-shirt. If you play on their basketball team, you get to wear one just like this. This shirt would let everyone know that you had made the team. What do you suppose you have to do to get on that basketball team, boys and girls? *(Let them answer.)* That's right. You would have to try out for it. But before you tried out for the team, you would practice very hard, wouldn't you? *(Let them answer.)* What would you have to do to get yourself ready for the basketball team? *(Let them answer.)* Yes. You would practice making baskets and you would try to become very quick on your feet. Do you think that jogging every day would help you get ready for the team? *(Let them answer.)* Yes. It would. Would you have to watch what you eat and drink so that you wouldn't be too fat? *(Let them respond.)* You sure would! You would have to eat good foods that give you lots of energy. Then — after all of your practicing and exercising, you would go and try out for the team. After everyone had tried out, the coach would probably read all the names of those who had made the team. You would all get to wear this uniform and to play in the games. That would be fun, wouldn't it, boys and girls? *(Let them respond.)*

Did you know that there is a team of God's special people? *(Let them answer.)* These people did the things they were supposed to do to make the team. They listened to God's word and followed the teaching of Jesus. They weren't afraid to follow Jesus when he called them. The Bible says that their names are written in a huge book. Does anyone know what we call these people who are on God's special team? *(Let them answer.)* They are called saints! Because they answered God's call, they are now in heaven. Did you know that all of us have been called to be on that team, also, boys and girls? *(Let them respond.)* All of our names have been written in that great book that says we are on our way to heaven. Today we say "thank you" to the Lord for his special people — the saints. Let's ask him to help us become members of that great team, too. Will you do that, boys and girls? Good. God bless you. Amen.

45
You Are Chosen

For we know, brothers and sisters beloved by God, that he has chosen you.
— 1 Thessalonians 1:1-5a, v. 4

Object: A wedding ring

Good morning, boys and girls. Can you tell me what this is? *(Show them the wedding ring.)* That's right, it is a ring, but it isn't just any kind of ring. This one is very special. When a person puts this ring on, he or she becomes a different person! Can you guess why this ring is so special, boys and girls? *(Let them guess.)* This ring is a wedding ring. When a man puts this ring on a woman's finger, she becomes a new and wonderful person. She becomes that man's wife! Does anything else change in this woman's life, boys and girls? *(Let them answer.)* The woman usually gets a new last name — her husband's. Then she moves into a new home and starts living as Mrs. Smith or Jones or whoever. The man receives a ring, too. It makes him a husband; after he starts wearing this ring, his whole life is usually very different from what it was before. How do husbands and wives find each other, boys and girls? How did your mom and dad find each other? *(Let them answer.)* Just think, out of all the men and women in the world, one day your mother met your father and that was a special day. They probably went out on dates and talked to each other on the phone. Do you think that they wrote letters to each other? *(Let them answer.)* Yes, they probably did. People who like each other usually do write letters or send nice cards. Then one day your mom and dad made a big decision. They decided to get married. Out of all those people whom they had known or dated before, they chose each other. If they hadn't done that, you wouldn't be who you are today, would you, boys and girls? *(Let them respond.)*

Did you know that God did something like that for you and me? He chose us to be his special people. But God didn't have to choose only one person — lucky for us! He chose all of us. Since that day when God chose us, we have been new people, too. We received the name "Christian," and we are invited to come and worship in God's house as often as we want to . What was the important day when we become a member of this Christian family? *(Let them answer.)* The day of our baptism — that day was very much like your parent's wedding day. It made us new and beautiful people — God's children. Let's all thank God, today, for choosing us to be part of his family. Will you do that, boys and girls? Good. God bless you all. Amen.

46
Follow The Directions

And you become imitators of us and of the Lord...
— 1 Thessalonians 1:5b-10, v. 6

Object: A mixing bowl and chef's hat or apron, two spoons

Good morning, boys and girls. What do you suppose I am going to do with these things today? *(Hold up objects. Let them answer.)* Right. Looks like I'm going to do some baking. I thought that I would go home later today and mix up a big batch of chocolate chip cookies. Do you like chocolate chip cookies, boys and girls? *(Let them answer.)* Well, I really like them, too. When I was a boy, my mom used to make the best cookies in the world. No one's cookies ever tasted as good as my mom's! One day I told her that I wanted to learn how to make chocolate chip cookies that tasted as good as hers. So she let me help her. Mom put out all of the things I would need for the cookies. Can you guess what kinds of things I needed? *(Let them guess.)* Yes. I needed sugar, flour, baking powder, shortening, eggs, nuts — and of course the chocolate chips. I got to put everything into the bowl. Then my mother showed me how to mix it all up. She showed me how the batter should look before I put in the nuts and chocolate chips. Finally it was time to spoon the batter onto the baking tins. Mom took two spoons like this. *(Show them.)* and put some batter in one of them. Then with the other, she would scoop it out onto the baking pan. If I made the cookies too fat and sloppy, can you guess what would happen to them when they were finished baking? *(Let them guess.)* The whole pan would turn into one, big cookie! So I had to make each lump of batter not too big and not too small. Then we put the cookies into the oven, and Mom showed me how you could tell when they were finished baking. Those cookies tasted really good—because I did everything my mom told me to do.

Today Paul reminds us that being a Christian is a little bit like learning how to be a good baker or cook. We have to watch the people who are good Christians and try to live like they do. In the days when the Apostles were alive, everyone tried to live like they did. They showed the people how to live as Jesus wanted them to. Since the Apostles aren't around anymore, we have to find other people who will show us how Jesus wants us to live. Can you tell me which people are around today who can help us? *(Let them answer.)* Those are good answers, boys and girls. Let's all remember to follow the directions given to us by our parents, our teachers, our ministers and other good Christians so that we will turn out to be the best kinds of Christians we can be. Will you do that, boys and girls? Good. God bless you. Amen.

47
A Family Of Crooks

For as all die in Adam, so all will be made alive in Christ.
— 1 Corinthians 15:20-28, v. 22

Object: A sign to hang around someone's neck which says, "This person is a crook"

Good morning, boys and girls. How would you like it if you had to wear a sign like this all the time? *(Show them the sign. Let them respond.)* Do you know what a "crook" is, boys and girls? *(Let them answer.)* That's right. A crook is someone who probably can't be trusted because he lies or cheats or steals. Well, once there lived a man in a far-away country who did something very foolish. He stole the king's crown! It was a beautiful crown, made of gold and jewels. Well, this man didn't get very far, but before he was caught, he buried the crown in a safe place. The palace guards caught him and he was put in jail, but no one ever found the crown. Many years later, when the thief was very, very old, he was set free. But he had to wear this sign around his neck so that everyone would know what he had done. *(Hold up sign again. Place it around the neck of one of the children.)* That wouldn't have been a very nice sign to have to wear every day, would it, boys and girls? *(Let them respond.)* To really punish the man, the king decided that his children would have to wear it also. Then everyone would know that they belonged to the family of a crook. Even the man's grandchildren and great-grandchildren and great-great-grandchildren would have to wear it! Finally, many years later, a king came to the throne who decided that this family had suffered long enough because of what their relative had done so long ago. So this king forgave them all! He decided to forget it ever happened. The king said that none of those children and grandchildren and great-grandchildren of the crook had to wear that sign any longer. The king would have a new crown made. He would pay for it himself. That king must have been a very nice man, don't you think so, boys and girls? *(Let them respond.)*

Did you know that we also had a relative who got us all into trouble when he took something that didn't belong to him? Who was that, boys and girls? *(Let them tell you.)* Right. It was Adam! All of the people who lived after Adam had to wear the sign of sin on their souls — until God sent his Son to set us all free. Jesus got rid of the sign we all wore. Not only did he set us free — he helped us to become God's own children. Let's thank God today for sending us Jesus, who saved us from the sign of sin and showed us how to live new and beautiful lives. Will you do that, boys and girls? Good. God bless you. Amen.

48
A Friend Indeed

God is faithful; by him you were called into the fellowship of his Son, Jesus Christ our Lord.
— 1 Corinthians 1:3-9, v. 9

Object: A screwdriver, knife, pack of cigarettes, pile of money

Good morning, boys and girls. You are probably wondering what I am doing with all of these things! Well, I want to tell you a story about a boy named Billy. Some people used to call him "Bad-Boy Billy" because he was always in trouble! For instance, Billy would use this screwdriver to pry the hubcaps off cars! He loved to steal as many as he could. Then he would use this knife to slash tires because he thought that was great fun. Billy especially liked to slash the tires of people who gave him trouble — like his teachers, or the minister of his church, or the grumpy guy down the block. What do you suppose Billy's parents did when they found out about Billy's bad deeds, boys and girls? *(Let them answer.)* Yes, they punished Billy, and told him that he would have to earn the money to pay for new tires or hubcaps. But Billy didn't care. He kept right on doing bad things, which was why people called him "Bad-Boy Billy." One day Billy did something that was much worse than anything he had ever done before. Some older guys invited him to go along with them to rob a store. They thought that they could each get lots of money, like this. *(Hold up money.)* So Billy went along with them. When they got to the store, they told Billy to stay in the car and watch to see if anyone was coming. So Billy did, but after waiting quite a while, he decided to go into the store and see what was going on.

There he saw the older guys beating up the owner of the store. Billy tried to stop them but it was too late. The man later died. Poor Billy ended up having to go to prison to serve a long sentence. Isn't that a sad story, boys and girls? *(Let them respond.)* What do you think Billy's parents said to him after he got into so much trouble? *(Let them guess.)* Well, his parents told him that they would always love him, even though they didn't like what he did; they promised to visit him in prison as often as they could. And they did. Billy found out that his mom and dad were the best friends he ever had. When Billy finally got out of prison, he was a much older man, but he never forgot his wonderful parents.

We all know that God is an even better friend to us than anyone else in this world. Like our parents, he sticks with us, even when we get into trouble; he loves us, even when we turn our back on him. Today, let's all thank God for his friendship and especially for sending us Jesus to be our Savior and brother. Will you do that, boys and girls? Good. God bless you. Amen.

49

Watch For The Lord

But the day of the Lord will come like a thief...
— 2 Peter 3:8-14, v. 10

Object: A flashlight, rope, screwdriver, bag

Good morning, boys and girls. I want to show you what I have in this bag. *(Take out each item and hold it up.)* What kind of a person would need a bag like this? *(Let them guess.)* Well, a thief would probably need a bag full of tools like this. Why would a thief need a flashlight? *(Let them guess.)* Right. A thief usually comes at night, so he needs to be able to see where he is going. What would he use this screwdriver for? *(Let them answer.)* Yes, he would probably use this to pick the lock on the door so he could get into the house. Why would he need to have this rope? *(Let them tell you.)* Sometimes, a really nasty thief will tie up the people in the house. A thief might also use this rope to get out of a window if he had to. Of course, this bag would be important because the thief could put whatever he steals into it. The scariest thing about people who steal is that they often do it during the night when everyone is asleep. Sometimes a thief can break into a house and take what he wants without waking anyone up! Because thieves are usually sneaky people, they have a way of knowing when a family is going to be away on vacation or gone for the day. As soon as a family is gone, a thief can start doing his job because then no one will bother him.

Today you will hear one of our Scripture readings use the word "thief." Peter says that the Lord will come again to visit the world. But the day of his coming will sneak up on us just like a thief, sneaking up on a family at night. Peter is saying that Christians need to be awake; they need to keep their eyes open for that special day. Just like a family watches over its house so that no one can break into it, so Christians need to keep their eyes open each day, because one of those days will be the day that the Lord comes again. During Advent we are all getting ready to remember something special that happened long ago. What was that, boys and girls? *(Let them tell you.)* Right. Christ's *first* coming among us. But during Advent we also think about Christ's *second* coming, because we all want to be ready for that, too. The next time you hear about a thief breaking into a house, remember Peter's words — Christ will come when we aren't expecting him. So let's be ready! God bless you, boys and girls. Amen.

50
Test Everything

...but test everything; hold fast to what is good.
— 1 Thessalonians 5:16-24, v. 21

Object: Four candy bars, without the wrappers, cut into very small, bite-size pieces

Good morning, boys and girls. Did you ever see those television commercials where some person is asked to try out three or four different kinds of pop? *(Let them respond.)* Does the person know what kinds of pop he is drinking? *(Let them respond.)* No, he doesn't because the labels are all covered up. Of course, the person always chooses the right brand of pop so that the commercial can tell everyone how wonderful it is. Well, today I am going to let you take part in a little test that is something like that one. I have here four different kinds of candy, but without the wrappers. I am going to ask for some volunteers to help me decide which is the best candy bar. When we decide, then we'll get rid of the ones that aren't so good and buy some more of the ones we like. Who would like to help me out? *(Ask several children to try each one.)* Well, what do you think, boys and girls? Which candy bar is going to win the prize? *(Let them decide which is the best one. Then tell everyone what kind it is.)* Very good. Thank you for helping me do that little test on this candy.

That kind of test is sort of fun, isn't it? We could do that same kind of test with other things, too, couldn't we? We could test ice cream, cereal, soda pop, cookies. What other things could we test, to see which is the best? *(Let them give you some ideas.)* Those are good ideas. When your dad goes out to buy a car, he tests lots of different ones before he chooses the one that is best for him and for the family. If you were going to go out and buy a bicycle, you would probably try out several different models to see which one felt the best to you.

Today we will hear Paul telling us that we should do the same kind of testing with people who say that they have special gifts from God. Some of them might just be trying to fool us. Paul also says that we should test things that people ask us to do. Some of those things might not be so good, so we shouldn't do them. But those things which pass the Lord's test are always good to do. As we get ready for Christmas, let's remember to get our souls ready also by testing all those things we do each day. By getting rid of things that aren't pleasing to God, we will be in fine shape to say "happy birthday" to Jesus on his special day. Will you all try to remember these things, boys and girls? Good. God bless you. Amen.

51

Keep Your Soul In Shape

Now to God who is able to strengthen you according to my gospel and the proclamation of Jesus Christ...
— Romans 16:25-27, v. 25

Object: A big bottle of vitamins, box of Wheaties, jar of peanut butter

Good morning, boys and girls. How is everyone today? Are you getting excited about Christmas? It will be here before we know it! I'll bet your mothers and fathers have been so busy that they could use some of the things I brought with me today. *(Hold up and name the items.)* Why do we take vitamins, boys and girls? *(Let them tell you.)* That's right. Vitamins help us when we are young to grow into healthy men and women. When we are adults, vitamins give us energy and keep us healthy, too. They give us strength to do our work. Baseball and football players, swimmers and runners, probably take a lot of vitamins, don't you agree, boys and girls? *(Let them respond.)* They probably eat a lot of Wheaties, too. Do you know any famous people who eat Wheaties so that they will have strength to be good athletes? *(Let them tell you.)* Some people also eat lots of peanut butter because it is full of protein. Peanut butter helps some people get more energy. Do you eat peanut butter, boys and girls? *(Let them tell you.)* We ordinary people need a little help getting enough energy and strength to do all the jobs we have to do each day. It is nice to have strong bodies; that's why most of us will eat our vitamins and Wheaties. We will even eat vegetables we don't like and keep away from foods that are bad for us — just so we will be strong and healthy. Some people also exercise every day, too, so that their bodies will be in good shape.

Well, today Paul talks to us about getting our souls in good shape. Will vitamins help our faith? *(Let them tell you.)* No, not even Wheaties and vegetables and peanut butter will make our faith strong. There is only one person who can help us to have strong faith — do you know who that is, boys and girls? *(Let them tell you.)* God himself. God sent us a great big dose of strength when he sent us Jesus, because Jesus helped us to know how God wanted us to live. That's why we are so thankful each Christmas Day. On that day, God shared a great big secret with us. On that day he sent us all the strength we will ever need to keep our faith in good shape. Let's thank him for that today. O.K., boys and girls? Good. God bless you. Amen.

52
God's Broadcasters

This is the message we have heard from him and proclaim to you, that God is light and in him there is no darkness at all.
— 1 John 1:1—2:2, v. 5

Object: Pictures of Tom Brokaw, Dan Rather, Willard Scott, or any other news broadcasters

Good morning, boys and girls. Do you know who these people are? *(Hold up the pictures.)* That's right. All of these people have the same kind of job. They are newspeople. They let us all know what is going on all over the world. All we have to do is turn on our television set at the right time, and we find out what is happening everywhere. These men and women are kind of like our direct line to the world. Remember when the big earthquake hit the Los Angeles area? *(Let them respond.)* These people went to work right away, didn't they? If you turned on your television or radio, you would have seen and heard about everything that happened to people in L.A. on that terrible day. Remember when a big oil tanker spilled its oil into the ocean? *(Let them respond.)* We could see the tanker struggling in the heavy seas and the beaches, birds, and animals coated with oil.* These reporters were all on the job. It's a good thing we have these special news teams, isn't it, boys and girls? *(Let them respond.)* They help us to know what is happening.

Sometimes I like to think of the men who wrote the books of the Bible as God's special news team. They wrote down all of those things that God wanted his people to know. The four men who wrote the Gospels told us all the news about the life of Jesus. What are the names of those four men who wrote the Gospels, boys and girls? *(Let them tell you.)* Matthew, Mark, Luke and John — we call them the evangelists. They each wrote about the life of Jesus. Each one of them told us special things about him. John had lots of wonderful things to say about Jesus. One of the things he said was that Jesus was the light of the world. When Jesus came into the world, he got rid of the darkness of sin. Jesus was full of the light of God. We should be thankful for people like John the Evangelist because they help us to know Jesus. All we have to do is open the Bible or listen to the readings each Sunday, and we will learn something new. Let's listen carefully today to the special messages John has for us. Will you do that, boys and girls? Good. God bless you. Amen.

*You may use any current event applicable in your situation in place of these examples: i.e., extended severely cold weather, major fire, hurricane damage, etc.

www.ingramcontent.com/pod-product-compliance
Lightning Source LLC
Chambersburg PA
CBHW071718040426
42446CB00011B/2124